CA

Richmond upon Thames Libraries

Renew online at www.richmond.gov.uk/libraries

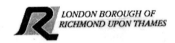

LONDON BOROUGH OF
RICHMOND UPON THAMES

I WENT FOR A WALK

I WENT FOR A WALK

GABRIEL STEWART

Unbound Digital

This edition first published in 2019

Unbound

6th Floor Mutual House, 70 Conduit Street, London W1S 2GF

www.unbound.com

© Gabriel Stewart, 2019

ISBN (eBook): 978-1-91261-897-2
ISBN (Paperback): 978-1-91261-896-5

Cover design by Mecob

Printed and bound in Great Britain by Clays Ltd, Elcograf S.p.A.

Thank you to Darcy, Flo and my parents for everything you did for me throughout this year off.

Dedicated to Ken and Gill, my grandparents, for believing in me and playing a huge part in making this happen.

Dear Reader,

The book you are holding came about in a rather different way to most others. It was funded directly by readers through a new website: Unbound.

Unbound is the creation of three writers. We started the company because we believed there had to be a better deal for both writers and readers. On the Unbound website, authors share the ideas for the books they want to write directly with readers. If enough of you support the book by pledging for it in advance, we produce a beautifully bound special subscribers' edition and distribute a regular edition and e-book wherever books are sold, in shops and online.

This new way of publishing is actually a very old idea (Samuel Johnson funded his dictionary this way). We're just using the internet to build each writer a network of patrons. Here, at the back of this book, you'll find the names of all the people who made it happen.

Publishing in this way means readers are no longer just passive consumers of the books they buy, and authors are free to write the books they really want. They get a much fairer return too – half the profits their books generate, rather than a tiny percentage of the cover price.

If you're not yet a subscriber, we hope that you'll want to join our publishing revolution and have your name listed in one of our books in the future. To get you started, here is a £5 discount on your first pledge. Just visit unbound.com, make your pledge and type STEWART19 in the promo code box when you check out.

Thank you for your support,

Dan, Justin and John
Founders, Unbound

Super Patrons

Roy Ackerman
Jane Ashley
Andrew Austwick
Dawn Austwick
Malcolm Austwick
Ryan Baldi
Sabina Barbato
Aidan Barker
Gina Barker
Isobel Barker
Liam Barker
David Barnett
Samuel Berlin
Jenny Boyce
Harry Brewer
Asa Butterfield
Ailsa Carson
Christine Cocker
Abby Coppard
Michael Cordner
John Crawford
Darcy Dixon
Shirli Ender Buyukbay
Clare Fermont
Jack Forey
Barbara Frost
Isobel Gage
Julie Gallagher
Tom Galloway
Annie Hagman
Halifax College
Nick Henman

Lewis Jackson
Naomi Johnson
Liam K
Sabita Kumari-Dass
Sara Llewellin
Alice Lloyd-Davies
Yvonne Maddox
Kamran Mallick
Evelyn Marr
Sam Mathias-Stanley
Fiona Millar
Jamie Noel
Ella Potter
Gareth Quarry
Bedford Sparrow
Rebecca Stewart
Selena Stewart
Lucy Stout
Asa Stuart
Miriam Stwt
Richard Sumray
Bertie Tucker Hough
Bibiana Wigley

Contents

Contents

Prologue

Most People go to Asia in their Gap Year...

It is 10 February 2016 and I am walking down the winding country roads of Sussex, letting my head-torch lead me through the unlit path ahead. Little white drops begin to fall around me. Confused, I look up to see if a tree has blossomed early, spraying its glimmer of hope for summer onto the soul wandering below. No. It has started to snow. I stand for a second, bewildered. It isn't cold enough to snow. I mean, yes there are the mini mist-clouds emerging from my mouth every time I decide to let a breath out, but surely I'd at least have to *feel* a bit cold myself for it to be cold enough to snow.

I stumble onwards as the searing pain in my ankle re-emerges to remind me what a twat I was for committing to walk 1,000 miles in my gap year. This is day two. I have approximately 955 miles to go. At this moment, the idea of lying in the cushioned sand of a sun-streaked beach feels very attractive to me. Then I could claim that I had experienced, and embraced, the culture of the beautiful country I was visiting as I lay next to my fellow white middle-class Europeans, all feeling the same spirit inside them.

I am not bashing it. I mean, by all means go ahead and join the tens of thousands of late teens as they enjoy their drink- and drug-fuelled months exploring the 'fascinating' world of Southeast Asia. But don't for one second claim you are 'experiencing' and 'embracing' the culture of such areas. You are not. You are following a tour created with the sole purpose of allowing you to entertain these thoughts in your head while making sure that you do not actually touch this culture with your destructive Western hands. How many of the backpackers who have trampled through Bali have learnt about or even heard of the brutal genocide of over a million communists in Indonesia? Or the fact that the same people who committed the atrocities remain in positions of power today? I'm not claiming any moral high ground against the people of Indonesia, by the way, as the US and quite likely the UK were fully involved in such atrocities and still pride themselves on being allies and trade partners of Indonesia's wondrous government. My point is that it is not possible to explore a country's culture by passing through it for less than a month. You are simply on holiday, a reasonably long holiday.

I think you can guess why I didn't go 'travelling' in my gap year.

Instead I decided to walk, and walk quite a bit at that. A while back, I – that is, my sixteen-year-old self – was sitting on a train staring out of the window, probably acting out a music video in my head. The stare into the distance accompanied by the generic pout representing a thousand emotions. You know it. Anyway, as I stared I realised, pretentious as it sounds, that I wanted to be on the other side of the glass, walking, exploring, and just generally seeing the country at close quarters. So, fast forward three years and here I am in my nineteenth year, walking across that same country... and wondering why I committed myself to this idiotic act. Of course, cool as it sounds, I didn't just up sticks and wander off into the sheep-filled British landscape. There was a fair bit of planning along the way, as well as earning a bit of money from children with boomerangs. But we'll get on to that later.

First, there's the all-important question. Why was I doing this? The question that has a thousand answers yet I couldn't seem to find the right one. I've been asked that question a million times, and asked myself the same question a million more. Why would anyone commit themselves to walk over 1,000 miles for no particular reason? I can easily bat away strangers with the answer 'it's for charity', but in truth I only decided to do it for charity a few months before I started. So, no, I am not doing this because I am a wonderful person who, in every bone of my body, is driven by the desire to do good. I set off not really knowing the answer to the question. But gradually, as I went along, I began to realise what the answer was.

Boomerangs and Beginnings

August 2015 to January 2016

It's mid-August. I'm lying in bed the morning after celebrating my eighteenth birthday in style (in the grottiest club in Dalston, wearing a necklace proudly announcing my age to my fellow clubbers). I now need a job. So, I get up and set off on my bike. Next I am wandering down Church Street hoping that they'd love to have a local middle-class boy to greet their local middle-class customers. First interview goes well: 'I mean, so you don't really have any experience, do you?' is a lovely way to instil confidence in a person. In all honesty, he could probably detect the signs of my struggle to cycle to the interview having drowned myself in alcohol nine out of the previous eleven nights.

A hundred CVs later, I am waiting to be interviewed for my 'dream job' (I lied in my covering letter). The job is that of a toy demonstrator... well, actually a boomerang demonstrator. I stumble my way through the interview, and the subsequent training, where the boomerang probably hits my face more times than it lands in my hands. Yet for some reason they still decide to employ the uncoordinated oaf in front of them. I mean, the concept of catching a boomerang while trying to sell what is essentially a piece of foam to children makes me shit myself (just to clarify, I did not actually spread faeces across the shop floor). But after you've thrown a boomerang for over seven and a half hours a day you kind of get the hang of it, although that didn't stop me mauling hundreds of children in the process (with my foam boomerang, I mean).

Job sorted, apart from the occasional screaming woman, and a manager who doesn't like the idea of foam boomerangs flying around his shop, as if he hadn't realised that he was managing a toy store.

Why did I need said job? Well, aside from the regular reason of requiring money for general survival, I was soon to depart on a colossal trek and having some funds for this would be rather helpful. So, now that I had a full-time job, planning how on earth I would complete the trek would probably be a good next step...

I wanted to walk across the UK with just a backpack, camera and tent for company. That was the extent of the plan at this point. Oh, and the small fact that I would be attempting to follow the railways as closely as possible along the way. That might be slightly important information. I'm not obsessed with trains, by the way; I feel I should point that out. There was a slightly saner, if a tad peculiar, reasoning for it. I wanted to document the countryside that whizzes past you as you look out at it from the comfort of your train seat. Essentially, it was to be a photography project that would present a view of Britain from the perspective of its railways. 'A View from a Train' was one of the many shit titles I had envisioned for the photography book I planned to create from the experience. The fact that you are not currently reading a photography book probably tells you that plans did change a fair bit. For now, though, the railways of Britain would be my guide to exploring it.

So, I grabbed my laptop and started, quite randomly, searching differing distances between cities and towns on Google Maps. I had decided that the trip would take place as a series of journeys, not just an endless ramble across the countryside. I would start in one place – most of the time that starting place would be London – and finish in another, then return home, on the same train line I had just followed, for a few days of rest. After countless hours of research, I chose to begin my trip with a respectable 60-mile walk from London to Brighton. This was not because of any particular affiliation with the city of Brighton. I mean, I had a few friends who were there at uni and they were all right but they weren't a good enough reason to walk sixty miles – no offence guys. The reason was distance. I needed a solid chunk of miles to build up from and Brighton represented an opportunity for that. I could also stay at a mate's house upon arrival which is always nice.

I then set out on planning journeys that would gradually

increase in length from this starting point, some of which involved destinations and train routes I had often travelled to and on for various reasons, like London to Bath and Birmingham (family). Others, like that between Settle and Carlisle, were simply because of their reputed beauty. And an awful lot were just because they fitted into the right mileage to build up my stamina for my final treks to Penzance and Edinburgh from, you guessed it, London. Why Edinburgh and Penzance? To my knowledge at the time, they were the furthest you could go from London on a direct train. So, as it seemed as if I was planning to endlessly punish myself, I thought I'd have a go at walking to them.

In the midst of all this planning I had settled on twenty miles a day being a reasonable target to aim for. How wrong I would be... Not aware of my naivety, I began calculating the number of days each journey would take: three for Brighton; four to five for Folkestone; seven for Bath. The list went on and the durations increased. Campsites were found and, where campsites couldn't be found, possible wild camping spots. I was rather enjoying it. Plotting out all the details of the plans. Playing around with the dots on Google Maps so that I could attempt to be as close to the train lines as possible.

This is where the dream of re-enacting *Stand By Me* began to fall apart. Walking right next to the tracks wasn't exactly feasible unless I wanted to desert the footpaths and trample through random farmers' fields. I had to compromise. I would make sure I was always within a reasonable distance of the railway but would not seriously inconvenience myself just for the sake of sticking as close to it as possible. Looking back, this was probably the moment my photography plan changed from documenting the view from a train window to documenting my actual journey and the countryside that accompanied it.

I realise that giving you all that history of the planning stage still hasn't really addressed *why* I was doing this whole trek thing. It explains what I hoped to use it for in the future, but not why I had chosen to spend my 'gap year' doing something so at odds with normality.

In truth, as I've said, I wasn't entirely sure myself. Despite this, I will attempt to provide you with a little (or extremely long) explanation as to the reasoning behind my taking on such an idiotic challenge. For months, I would tell myself that it was because I wanted to explore the UK before I travelled to other parts of the world, via train of course. This wasn't true. It was a good line, like the charity one. But it was another made-up line to provide a sufficient answer to the question: why was I doing this insane stupid weird thing on what was meant to be my year off? Well, people didn't exactly phrase it like that, but you could tell that was the general gist behind the veil of politeness with which they greeted my account of the plan.

I suppose one reason was that I'm one of those people who when they commit to doing something cannot betray that commitment – I will fight through it until the pain is so desperate that I have no choice but to end the self-inflicted torture. It's idiotic, I know. But the guilt that climbs into my mind is too great to ignore. If I do not do what I say I am going to do, I will have fallen on my own sword. And the sword which has severed my insides would prevent me from enjoying the day-to-day life that I *wish* to enjoy. Breaking such a commitment is not about the opinion others will have of me (well it is a little bit, but shush that for now); it is more about the betrayal of my own self. I would have failed to complete a challenge I had set for myself and therefore let my past self down.

What I'm saying is that I was walking across the UK partly because I had committed myself to the twattish trek, so I could not now turn my back on this hefty challenge. Believe me, I do see a certain lack of real logic behind everything that I am saying right now. There isn't much logic in most of life though, is there? And it's still rather good most of the time. Of course, I really did crave the experience of hiking across the windswept hills that I normally only gazed upon while sitting in the comfort of a fast-moving metal box. There was some desire – it wasn't all just a will to prove to myself and all the fuckers out there that I could do it. You fuckers, you know who you are.

Anyway. Another reason. Originally, it seemed like a solid plan for the future. It would be fun. Painful? Walking across the UK? Not a chance. Bear in mind that I was in my first year of A levels, so my year off before uni seemed a fair distance away. This meant it was one of those plans/ideas that you have in the back of your mind. It didn't matter that I wasn't 100 per cent sure how I would do it. It was far away. I had the slightly more important issue of my A levels to worry about: probably better to try and decrease the chance of a psychological breakdown, not increase it. I would have six months or so to figure out the actual plan after I had put the devil's porridge of A levels behind me. So, it was more a dreamy prospect that hung about in the distant desert, and the logistics and twattishness of the commitment would not have to be dealt with until later.

Then 'later' arrived. My 'gap year' had started. I would probably have to confront the elephant in the room. I didn't fully understand what I had proudly declared I was doing to every individual who came within earshot of me. I guess the inner romantic within me had glossed over the reality of walking across depressingly bleak moors in rainstorms by replacing them with images of rolling hills illuminated by the setting sun and horses galloping into the distance, while I sat on the side of a hill I never knew existed and gazed out upon the beauty that surrounded me.

But it was a genuine wish to explore the unknown that really did tempt me. The lack of a strict *reason* behind what I was doing excited me: I would wander the countryside doing whatever I wanted; I would stay in one town for a few days if it intrigued me. Visit the local pub; the local shop; speak to local people; just gain a sense of ordinary life in other places. Explore. That was the word. I wanted to *explore*. It goes all the way back to the pretentious reasoning I had originally given my plans. That we spend so much time watching – from a car, from a train – the country we live in whizz past. I had been granted the gift of a year where I had no goals to reach, nothing to strive for. I had the time to explore. So why shouldn't I? Why shouldn't I get off that train and walk out into the world which I had stared at countless times from the other side of a pane of glass? I wanted to explore the country I had been born into. That's all. And of course that wasn't just a chore I felt like I had to complete simply because I had committed to it. And it wasn't some sort of endurance activity to impress those around me. I wanted to have fun. I wanted to do things I never would do otherwise; I wanted to meet people I never would otherwise. Most of all, I wanted to have these weird quirky experiences in these weird quirky places that I would never forget. That was it. That was why I had signed myself up to something that sounded so insane. Because it didn't sound so insane to me.

A chore. That is the thing I wished it wouldn't become. But it did. Slowly the dreamy sense of the unknown disappeared. Replaced by months of thorough planning. Every road would have to be researched, every one of my walks would be a 'journey' and every 'journey' would have to have a starting point and a final destination. I tried for a long time to figure out where my downfall came from.

Charity. That's where. The dark, self-denying reasoning behind my straying from enjoyment could be laid at the door of my sense of obligation to do this thing in the name of charity. I couldn't just say I was going to stroll off into the countryside and expect people to sponsor me for what would basically be me wandering about for six months. Doing something for charity necessitates the impressiveness factor, the sacrifice factor, the idea that, because you are doing it for charity, the something has to be stunningly impressive, something that causes you pain, not something that you enjoy. So the idea of people sponsoring me to go and stay in a random town for a few nights sounded a bit ridiculous to me. I would have to wow people with plans for much more challenging walks to faraway places like Edinburgh and Penzance – without actually thinking about the consequences of making such commitments.

The good thing about doing something for charity is that it means you can't back out of it. The bad thing is that it often saps the enjoyment out of it – I couldn't dreamily wander the UK without a care in the world any more. I would have to make a schedule because now people would be watching and expecting me to achieve these incredible feats. It became more about something that I now *had* to do rather than something that I *wanted* to do. It had become a chore, the unholy word which I wished never to utter in relation to my walks. All I wanted to do was wander the villages, towns and cities that embodied the UK at my own pace in my own way. At first the planning had been fun. Now the whole thing was threatening to become this *over*-planned venture which I no longer felt excited by. I didn't want to have a set final destination, I didn't even always want to know where I was staying that night. I just wanted to wander.

Charities are great. Don't get me wrong. They do wonderful things both nationally and globally for millions of people. Renewable World promotes the things I believe in more than anything else: renewable energy and combating climate change. It was perfect. The slight fall in public trust that charities have undergone meant that I did my fair share of research in order to be sure that Renewable World did what they said on the tin. They did. So, I decided. I would walk across the UK in aid of Renewable World. But my advice now is, if you're considering doing something a bit different that might be seen as weird or odd like I was, don't then decide to do it for charity simply because of the fact it is weird or odd. The constant question 'Are you doing it for charity?' was the first hurdle I fell at. Instead of confidently proclaiming, 'No, I'm doing it for myself', I let my conscience get in the way and whimperingly responded with, 'Oh yeah that's a good idea'. You fucking twat. You should've just done what you wanted to do.

Oh well. I decided to walk in the name of Renewable World, and I'd have to deal with the consequences. Now I needed to do a bit of training for the walks. This was a bit of a struggle. I had confidently announced that I would start training in September so that by February walking would be second nature. By mid-October I'd walked a grand total of about five miles as practice. Not exactly going to plan. But then came the 'Great Walk to the University of Hertfordshire' – really rolls off the tongue, doesn't it? Twenty miles in one day. The challenge was set. I grabbed my fellow pioneers, my friends Sam and Ellis, to set off across the beautiful expanse of suburban London. Our friends Tung and Joime would await us at the finish line with the promise of a floor to sleep on. Three miles in, my back felt like it had been scraped across cobbled ground before being slammed into submission by an overexcited baby ogre. Fifteen miles later we stood, confused, by the side of an unlit motorway where the pitch-blackness pretty much summarised our moods, especially as Sam had just been assaulted by nettles and accompanied his pain with the occasional yelp of 'Fuck!' or 'Shit!' or even 'Fuckity fuck!' We'd been told to go down a path through what looked like a forest. You can't really tell, though, when even the sun's given up hope and the moon hasn't bothered to turn up. A man we spoke to, who was illuminated by a fire burning in front of his feet, told us to take the first left turn and stick to the stone path. The stones disappeared soon after we started walking...

Anyway, eventually we retraced our steps, found our way, and collapsed onto the campus shuttle bus. We stumbled into our friends' rooms drenched in sweat and mud.

Showered up and feeling fresh, I stupidly decided to go out: Tung supplied me with the match to set my night of alcoholic beverages alight. The University of Hertfordshire's one and only club is an odd one. A highly segregated one may be a more fitting description. The ground floor, playing your typically tragic poppy chart music, was filled by a largely white audience. The floor above, playing a mix of grime, hip-hop and R&B, was filled by a largely black audience. This may have just been about musical taste, but the white guys sitting in the corner of the top floor sure were keen on pointing it out. It's always a strange night when someone proudly asks you to 'join the white people'...

After dancing through this weirdly segregated club we stumbled home, road sign in hand, to the tune of the clock striking four. Looking back I don't really understand why I decided to get pissed out of my head after walking twenty miles, especially when I picture myself asleep in Tung's kitchen at 4am surrounded by his bemused friends, but hey, I do things. Hung-over, aching all over, struggling to walk: the next morning felt great! My hope of training on the weekends and working on the weekdays was slowly disappearing with every boomerang I threw.

Another slight change of plan. Walking and working seemed to create a new endangered species: my feet. So walking just five or six miles every weekend until I could say goodbye to the boomerangs in December seemed like a better plan. I could then fully destroy myself by training throughout January, because cramming four months of training into one month sounded like a great idea. (It wasn't.) But on to that in a bit; first we have the months of my residing in The Rochester Castle to get through. I don't live in a castle by the way. The Rochester is a Wetherspoons, a cheap chain of pubs for those of you who have not had the pleasure of entering one. It's basically the only place anyone under twenty-five can afford to drink in London without blowing half their wages in one night. Slurping; sipping; dancing; boogying; shouting; screaming. You name it and I would be doing it at the Roch three nights a week; class did not feature in this period of my life. A high point has to be the experience of eating breakfast in the Roch nine hours after we'd been – slightly – intoxicated there. What are gap years for, eh?

Slip in a few trips, to Brighton, Bournemouth and Paris, and that's November and December covered. Brighton and Bournemouth were alcohol-aided trips to my mates at uni. I'd like to quickly clarify that I don't actually drink huge amounts, despite this book pointing to the opposite. I do often end up the drunkest person at the party, especially when the party's in the Roch, but the regularity of such drunkenness is not as great as this book may have you believe. Just thought I needed to clear that up.

Alcohol did also find its way into the Paris trip. But Paris was about something more important: the climate summit. I haven't, surprisingly, dwelt on this so far, but I'm basically a reasonably impassioned climate activist. I feel like calling myself an activist is slightly pretentious and probably overstates the extent of my activism, but my position is simple and easy to understand. The

Paris talks were huge, billed as the final chance to make a shit situation not dreadfully shit, just reasonably shit. Off I trotted onto the Eurostar, across the Channel, with my friends Ellis and Rivka briefly by my side before they wandered off to their comfy cosy flat while I trudged off to a warehouse infested by fellow climate activists. I accidentally sat down among a group of people with the assumption that none of us really knew each other. *They* knew each other, they *all* knew each other. As the realisation sank in that I was a sloth latched onto this tree of friendship, so did the awkwardness. I burrowed into my sleeping bag camouflaged behind a book to show that I didn't wish to penetrate their circle of trust as dozens more of them surrounded me with their friendly awkward smiles hiding bewilderment about who I was. I just wanted to sleep, forget it all and fuck off to yoga in the morning.

Twenty-four hours later, I am sitting amongst my own friends as a mix of pre-pubescent teens and middle-aged ravers dance away to the strange contrast of tracks offered up by the Friends of the Earth 'disco'. Jackson 5 then Skrillex is always a good combo. Pretty much sums up the weirdness-and-wonderfulness of the trip. We were then soothingly serenaded back by a softly spoken man and his friendly guitar on the otherwise silent Metro. In contrast to my friends, who had joined me in the ecosphere of the hippity-hop warehouse, I slept like a baby in preparation for the big day of protest ahead. Friends of the Earth started off the day by living up to their billing of creating the least controversial protest possible in which they spelt out the words 'climate justice' across the city via the use of social media. Then came the more adventurous blocking of the road leading to the Arc de Triomphe. Twenty thousand red protestors drew metaphorical red lines, with the aid of cloths, flowers, umbrellas, inflatable balls and more, to defy the ban on mass protest in France. There was something special about it. As we wandered through the Parisian streets in our thousands, bewildering the heavily armed and incredibly over-resourced French police, it felt as if a new, stronger movement was starting. The relative weakness of the

Paris deal wouldn't matter; that was expected. Building a stronger movement of direct action would be what created change and gave hope because we would be the ones fighting long after the 195 leaders of the world had left office. As world leaders failed to enshrine their already weak commitments into international law, we were the ones remembering the lives of the hundreds of thousands, perhaps millions, who have died because of climate change. We will therefore be the ones who will fight tooth and nail for the hundred million more threatened by climate change, and then for the next hundred million and the next. Because however much you think of climate activists or protestors in general as unemployed, lazy or idealistic twats, they are people driven by doing good, largely not for themselves but for others whom most often they do not know. Without people taking to the streets in protest almost every single one of the rights that we take for granted wouldn't exist today. So don't tell me that protesting is pointless.

Rant over. There may be a few more of those…

So Paris was good and, despite the many weaknesses in the agreement, 195 world leaders did manage to create a plan to combat climate change, agreeing on what was a pretty pointless statement: while they signed up to the principle of keeping the global surface temperature rise this century to well below 2°C, in reality the commitments that each country submitted as pledges would result in a 2.7°C temperature rise, according to scientists, and this commitment wouldn't be readdressed for five years. But hey it was better than Copenhagen.

Back to London and my final throwing of the almighty boomerang. I was finished! I would never have to throw a boomerang again! Until my dad informed me that I would have to teach the rest of my family as I had provided them with these delights for Christmas.

Proper walking training started. I would slowly raise the amount I walked by a mile each day so that I could walk the stupidly unrealistic total of seventeen miles a day by the end of the month. Training is genuinely awful. You're not actually doing the trek for real, so it's about inflicting pain upon yourself so that when you are doing it for real you'll be in a little less pain. If I'm honest, I had no idea what I was doing in training. I mean, I basically just went, 'I'm gonna be walking a while, so I should probably do some walking to practise. Yeah, that's a good idea, let's do some walking,' and off I walked. Nothing else, just walking; resting; walking; resting. No other exercise. Which may not have been the best of plans. I could proudly strut across the room at a party announcing that I'd walked the impressive total of fourteen to fifteen miles that day, to the awe of others at how seriously I was taking it. Yet, in reality, I was severely underprepared and out of my depth.

My plans to practise camping in my garden slowly disappeared with every fox poo that appeared in it. I had thought, of course, that camping in the garden of a terraced house, with daffodils on the one side and shrubbery on the other, was a fair equivalent to camping in the snow-topped peaks of the Lake District. The deafening screeches of foxes, as they found delectable nappies in bin bags, would prepare me for the sound of shotguns ending the lives of wandering pheasants. (But of course the countryside really is very different from the city. I guess there's positives and negatives on both sides. In the countryside, you can walk through a village and be greeted by every inhabitant, so that by the end of the walk you will know, among other things, that Ross, from Appletree Cottage, is sleeping with Susie, from Beechwood… However, you might also encounter a slightly racist or homophobic comment along the way, which always puts a bit of a downer on the occasion. Meanwhile in London, everyone sitting or standing around you is a stranger locked in their own world of iPhone, iPad or iPod with no communication with the people around them. But you can be safe in the knowledge that the majority of them aren't voting for UKIP and probably have reasonably PC views. So: friendly with dashes of xenophobia or closed off with a bit less xenophobia. Always a difficult choice.)

So, as I trekked through the darkest corners of Richmond, there was the small matter of equipping myself. I wandered off to Decathlon to 'research', which consisted of standing and staring at multiple waterproofs, confused at the apparent lack of difference. I didn't ask for help of course. I was ashamed to go grovelling back to the Decathlon workers after, naturally, rejecting their assistance, as a defence mechanism against their assaults on my entrance. The answer 'No, thanks' to the question 'Do you need any help, sir?' is now permanently ingrained in my brain to the point where even when help is very much needed, those words still spill out of my mouth ungratefully. There is no turning back; I could not possibly eat humble pie after slaying their hopeful faces with such brutal rejection. So I wandered on, the hopeless oaf, staring at camping cutlery, trying my hardest to look like I knew what I was doing: I needed to look like I knew my shit to justify the confidence with which I had shut down their offers of help. I realise now that I do inflict most of the pain and sense of failure that I feel on myself.

Ultralite; lightweight; petite; light; weightless; lite plus; lite minus. I never knew there were so many levels of light. If you ever decide to go hiking or do anything similar to it in your life, I warn you, do not go online, *do* just go to your local outdoor shop, and *do* ask the experts. Even if you have to throw water on the fire that is their desire to sell you the latest Gore-Tex raised webbed feet breathable shoe with a perfectly measured insole thrown in there. Online is a treacherous place. You cannot find a 'beginners to hiking' website – they do not understand the word 'beginners'. They assume that 'beginner' simply means you just take twenty days to climb a mountain instead of two. Not that you've never walked for longer than five hours in your life! I mean how am I supposed to know what a 'bathtub floor' of a tent is (well the name does describe a waterproofed floor quite well but, fuck off, that's not the point). Also, in reviewing tents, they talk about how a tent is good because you can add almost everything it doesn't have onto it. They call this tent perfect for a 'beginner', but a beginner is not going to be able to construct their tent like it is an assortment of loosely connected Lego blocks. The term 'beginner' is usefully used to describe someone who has no fucking clue what they are doing, not someone who could climb Mount Everest with a pitchfork.

In comes Sam, my wildebeest of a friend, whom you could quite easily believe grew up in Ray Mears's kangaroo pouch. He is the guy who watches that episode of *Survival with Ray Mears* on Travel Channel at 1am, yeah, the programme that you scroll past wondering which sane individuals watch it at 9pm, let alone 1am. So the rustic-born baby Sam could offer his advice on subjects ranging from bivvy bags to wild mushrooms – indeed, he's been on a multiple-day course on mushrooms (yes, 'multiple-day', you read it right). After thanking Christ for his birth during the acquiring of half my equipment, and after consultation with Sam and hiker forums, I stepped into the fearful terrain of Decathlon once again to conquer the ground I had tentatively stepped over a month earlier. Lamp, bought. Cooker, bought. Pans, bought. Dry bags, bought. Everything, bought. It was time for Epping. Now, if you're from North London you have probably heard of Epping Forest. It is the prime location for North Londoners to immerse themselves in woodland, in the ancient trees around them, in a desperate attempt to forget that they reside in a milieu of endless concrete for the other six days a week. Families, kinky couples and fucked-up teens. This is the place for their camping escapades. Sam and I would join them for a night.

First, we had to get there. The River Lea would be our guide (if you like a bit of Adele, yes, it's the same River Lea). I've never really understood why it was called a river. It is very much a canal. Well, it is decorated by canal boats and locks, usually the giveaway signs. I'm not going to search out what sort of waterway it actually is. I will enjoy the blissful ignorance I exist in. I like the endless internal debate I can have without Google or some wanker telling me some joyless factual explanation. Whatever it was, we would be walking alongside it for the majority of the sixteen or seventeen miles we'd be covering. The plan: walk to the forest; get there just before nightfall; find a place to settle down (preferably away from humans); have a chatter and a sleep; get up at sunrise; walk back; go to bed. It would be as close to the real thing as I would get. Sam would provide many tales of his experiences of doing the same journey with the largely white middle-class left-wing utopia that is Woodcraft Folk. He spoke of a view. A view, from atop a squelchy grassy hill, of the endless sprawl of London. A just reward for slowly ascending from this sprawl. Once this hill was reached, we would be looking back on the city we had left, with only a few miles to go to our destination.

Getting there. It wasn't the most challenging task. Aside from the faff on the way of attempting to cook some rice on a gas stove while hiding under a picnic table (it was raining), the day went relatively smoothly. I mean, walking along a flat canal path doesn't exactly sound like a dangerous death-defying experience. You're right, it wasn't. It was just a bit long. Walking past the soggy marshes of Tottenham; through the industrial setting of Edmonton; into the suburban black hole of Cheshunt to reach the sodden fields surrounding the tantalising M25. We reached the view, had a cheeky peek, and carried on. Now came the search for the forest. Sam would claim he knew exactly where we were going. That wasn't exactly true. After a few dead ends and incorrect forays into wooded areas, we eventually stumbled upon a place I recognised. A couple of years back, on the eve of starting sixth form, me and my mates decided to emulate the stereotype of getting fucked up in Epping Forest for a bit of fun. What crazy rambunctious teens we were. I hope you realise that's sarcastic. I'm not one of those people who blurt out unendingly annoying statements like 'I'm so weird' or 'I'm so crazy, you know'. If someone ever speaks those words, they are definitely not. So, back to the relevance of returning to my innocent pre soul-destroying-A-levels brain: we had accidentally stumbled across the campsite in which those frivolous activities had occurred. I now knew where to go. Ten minutes later, we'd be setting up camp.

Darkness descended. Sam lit his fire. Not on the ground! He had some weird fire thingy which gave you the desired warmth but did not cause a dot of damage to the grass or earth below. We sat resting on Sam's sleeping bag with the night sky taking hold at the wintry time of 4.30pm. We were tired, but sleep was to be many hours away. Conversation would have to do. Hours passed as we dissected every minute detail of our lives, friends and expectations for what was to come in the uncertain period that is university for both ourselves and the fabric of our friendship group. Yet, despite my willingness to endlessly chat away about whether our friendship group would crack and splinter because of the distances opening up within it, the chat became far from endless when the subject turned to me. Any attempt to have a meaningful conversation surrounding the subject of myself would be severed as soon as it raised its head. I could witter on with my embarrassing tales of drunkenness, yet when emotions became the topic I would shut down and enter hibernation until the emotional pressures subsided. Tactic: drop a hot piece of gossip. Topic changed. Success.

A mystical light in the distance started to confuse Sam. On edge, we turned off our torches. Was it a forest copper? I've forgotten what Sam called them so I'm gonna just call them forest coppers. Sounds shit but deal with it. I'm talking about the people who patrol public forests like Epping in case any mischief's going on, including wild camping. Essentially, we didn't want them to find us. Fines aren't the nicest thing in the world. After quietly whispering at one another for many minutes, we concluded that it was probably just a house. Well, we hoped. Sleep would be the best way to dispel the doubts so sleep we did.

Six am was announced by the gentle sounds of a Nokia alarm. Every inch out of my sleeping bag felt like another step into the icy wastes of Antarctica. I mean it was like 1°C so not exactly Antarctica but still fucking cold. After some prolonged faff we got out, packed everything down and began the trudge home. There was to be a lot of trudging ahead. Something Sam's feet definitely didn't want to hear. They had developed the charming company of a big ol' blister. Gently strolling along the canal to a comfy bed at home would no longer be an option. Occasional yelps of pain would come from his direction, as the fact that walking on a blister was not a lovely thing to do settled into his brain. I attempted to ignore my own pains as the cogs within my knees began to falter. It was the first time in all my practice walks that I actually felt like I was struggling. To be fair, it was the first time that I was actually doing something quite similar to the real thing. I guess it was what lay in store for the walking boy that was me. Great. I pootled on through the pain, nevertheless. Walking along the canal had begun to feel a bit too familiar. The never-ending industrial buildings or big open green expanses which might have been interesting if I hadn't seen them the day before. If you ever decide to do some idiotic walking thing like I did maybe don't do your long-distance practice walks to and fro over exactly the same route, a day after each other. Oh well, we'd done it now. On we trotted. Eventually Springfield Park would greet us, allowing us to banish the repetitive canal from our sight and dream of the familiar cosy beds that lay just over a mile away. Clamber up that hill (if you've been to Springfield Park, you know what I mean); glide down the final straight (well not so much gliding for Sam's blistered foot); drop Sam at his place; stumble home and jump into my bed wanting never to exit it again. I was dead. I'd only done two consecutive days of sixteen miles. In nine days I would be walking over twenty a day… I was maybe a bit more prepared than a baby bear was to fly a plane. So, not the most prepared. Bring it on, Brighton!

Brighton

February 2016

'Hit me, shoot me, someone injure me, so that I cannot do this any more, but won't be seen as giving up.' My thoughts of harming myself to escape the pain I was feeling provided me with some worry for what lay ahead; it was the first day. How could I walk to Edinburgh if I had struggled to reach the grand suburbia of Redhill? Surely, I had created a delusional fantasy that could not be realised. A fantasy that was self-inflicted. The pain was to be of my own making because I was the twat who had committed to walking across the UK.

Hours later, as I lay in my tent, full of Uncle Ben's finest rice and fluffy pancakes provided by the local vicar's wife (I'll get to that), I realised that I could do it. I knew it was going to be hard and painful but I just needed to bear through it and the reward would come. That was the first of many times that I had to fight my natural urge to jump on a train home and curl up in my bed until no one remembered what my gap year consisted of. But of course it wasn't going to be easy. More importantly, could it be enjoyable? I am not someone who simply wishes to inflict pain upon themselves in the name of 'endurance'. I am someone who wanted to escape from the city, enjoy the countryside, and have weird quirky experiences along the way. Fun, with all its childish connotations, was essential.

Fun is also a good way to describe the last night of drinking that took place before I descended onto the green plains of the English countryside. It began with the grand plan of reliving childhood memories while intoxicated at our childhood bowling alley, Rowans. Alcohol and bowling were always going to be an interesting combination. We start at Friday night dinner, my family's attempt at retaining our Jewish identity by celebrating the Shabbat with an array of vegetarian dishes and many of my friends. Indeed this is where I had my first sip of wine, both in my lifetime and on this individual evening. The honorary guests of the night were my friend Lukas and his parents. They sat, already tipsy from a few pints at the pub beforehand, joyfully engaging in political exchanges and family gossip across the candlelit table. Meanwhile, Lukas and I occasionally engaged in the conversation while filling our glasses up as often as possible because free alcohol was on the table and when free alcohol is put on the table, you drink it. (Don't always follow that advice by the way; it's not the best way to prevent being spiked.) We then tipsily stumbled out to be greeted by Juan buying a quarter-bottle of vodka at the shop. So, of course, our first thoughts were, let's get a quarter-bottle as well; again logic was not really in the equation at that minute. Quarter-bottled up, we headed to Rowans hoping to have drunk them by the time of our very jolly arrival. Mission completed.

I stumbled in, demanding they let the fifteen eighteen-year-olds in front of them into what they now called an 'over-twenty-one venue'. We got in! Drunkenness does have its advantages and confidence is one of them. So, there I stood, ready to grace our lane with its first ball while everyone hesitantly watched. I released the ball. But it was not our lane which was graced by the ball I had thrown. No. It was the one about three lanes down that was greeted by the beauty of my bowling skills. In shock, I turned round to the people I call friends to find them all hysterically laughing, so, as any sane drunken man would, I dropped to the floor and joined them. I just want to be clear that, although all of this is, as far as I know, true, it is not my own memory that I am reciting from: I have little to no recollection of the night after this point. The description of it has been donated by my dear friends. After falling to the floor, attempting to wiggle to my seat, and being dragged up by the same friends, I was left half conscious, sitting on the red bowling seats. I forgot to say that this was also largely thanks to Sam, the Bavarian bear I talked about before. He had given me many a double vodka and lemonade without my asking. This to the point where the alcohol was already down my throat before I had considered what I was doing. So, back to my half-conscious self. I proceeded to lather the floor and seats around me in the variety of vegetables, cheeses and nuts that I had consumed only a few hours before. At this point we realised it was probably time to leave, as did the security guards. I was then transported home via the assistance of a bus driver and the five-ton bulldozer he controlled. This was not without my vomiting again, this time on my friend Jack. I'm still sorry, Jack.

I woke up at 10am confused by my last memory of bowling and the fact that there was a note on me, saying, 'Call me in the morning, Darcy xx'. Not yet knowing that I had publicly humiliated myself in front of all my friends, I called her, and learnt about the events of the night that had led up to me being tucked into bed by my good mates, said Darcy and Jack. Thanks guys, I'll always owe you (especially Jack: sorry again).

... So, here we go. Tuesday 9 February, 6am. Awake, showered up and ready, I set off out of the door. Twenty miles to walk. Sixty miles in three days. Victoria station to Brighton station. Railway style. First decision: podcast; music; or nothing? I chose all three. Might as well experiment to find out what works best. Podcasts are good as long as you enjoy the podcast and are not pissed off by the pretentious sound of the voice in your ears. I'm sorry Hugh Fearnley-Whittingstall but I could not listen to you describe how food shapes our lives in this sort of fake 'radio voice'. I don't know how else to describe it. The voice where the speaker seems to be attempting to put emotions behind the lines they speak without actually feeling any such emotions. I'm guilty of it. I think pretty much everyone is. It's basically like Coldplay's music, trying so hard to be emotional that any emotions they had in the first place have disappeared from the record. That takes us into music. This is a difficult one. On the one hand, you want to listen to atmospheric music connecting you with the land around you. But on the other, you want to shut out the pain, forget what you are doing and engage with the music itself. Only upbeat or dance tracks can truly do that for me. Then there is the devilish option of no music and no podcasts. Nothing to protect my ears from the world around me! From the whistling wind ferociously smacking my ear to the gentle hum of traffic in the distance, reminding you that it is England and there is little chance of a complete escape from civilisation. Having no music scared me; the idea of having nothing to block out the pain of my backpack crushing my collarbone or my ankles slowly disintegrating into the ground below was frightening. I would succumb to the pain and therefore not be able to fight through the wall ahead of me. None of this was really the case of course: but unfortunately the fears embedded in me meant I didn't find out until later that walking without music actually creates opportunities for the uplifting experience of meeting and chatting to other people which I had craved.

Walking out of London has its benefits and drawbacks. Benefit: you see all walks of life going through their daily routines, which has the added advantage of providing more interesting photographs. A photo with an individual to focus on always offers a little more intrigue than an empty landscape. Drawback: the landscape isn't anywhere near as beautiful as the country especially when the main roads exiting London are what I just said, main roads, so are chock-a-block with cars and empty of character. Meaning that even with the individuals dominating the picture you do not get the beautiful landscape to accompany it. That being said, the principal pain is the fact that these main roads are never-bloody-ending. Walking down the same road for over two hours creates slight psychological problems. You feel as if you are making no progress and become paranoid about the time you are taking, questioning whether you will make it to your target before nightfall.

I didn't. Night was indeed falling as I crossed the M25 (on a bridge of course, not playing a literal version of the video game *Sheepish*). Although walking along an A road with no pavements, and multiple cars speeding past me every few seconds with the accompanying sounds of beeping horns, felt almost as horrible as I imagine crossing the M25 would be. Google Maps had fucked me over. I do understand that I was a right twat for relying on Google Maps for walking directions; every experienced hiker is probably hysterically laughing, reading this. Ordnance Survey (OS) maps were also in my travelling group so I was not the completely pathetic inexperienced hiker that you are imagining. But, of course, neither could inform me that such a road had no pavement to accompany it as it exited the metropolis of London into the detached-house suburbia of Reigate.

I have slightly skipped over my quite dramatic psychological breakdowns. My mind was not in the right place by 2.30pm on 9 February 2016. I wasn't sure if it was the overall lack of food I'd consumed as I attempted to follow the internet-provided idea of just intensely snacking throughout the day, or the sheer distance I'd covered as I trekked up another hill after already surpassing the twenty miles I had expected to do that day. Tears suddenly began to gush out of my eyes. The mud below me would explode into the air as my feet ferociously beat it to a pulp in frustration. The trees on either side didn't escape the beating either; my hands grabbed the nearest stick and began to assault these beings with what was basically one of their own limbs. Next they would be pounded by a set of impressive insults, such as 'You stupid fucking bugger twat!', which I feel were probably more aimed at myself than at the innocent bystanders around me. I did slightly calm down. But the final five miles of the day were then mainly dominated by phone conversations which I couldn't sustain because of my tendency to burst into tears or yelps of agony. My mum and Flo would be the grateful recipients of these delightful phone calls. Flo's one of my best mates, by the way, and even though she's experienced me at my worst we still haven't really spoken about those phone calls since. My attempts to quell such psychological torture by devouring a whole box of Jaffa Cakes failed miserably. So I wouldn't say I have the fondest memories of those few hours stumbling through the spitting rain to crawl into the vicarage. My arrival felt more like a relief than a celebration.

I should probably explain why I was camping in the garden of a vicarage in Redhill. It is not because I am a great believer in God – I am not – or a sinful man wanting to repent for his devilish actions – again, I am not. It is because of my mum. She had panicked at the fact that I had not found a wilderness to nestle my tent into and so had contacted a local vicar after her desperate call to arms on Facebook had failed. He, like I assume many vicars would, graciously agreed to offer an intrepid teenager his back garden to sleep in. John and his lovely wife greeted the muddy imbecile in front of them with open arms. I stripped off my layers of waterproofs, which were really to protect my actual clothes from mud rather than to shield them from rainwater, and collapsed onto their sofa while cradling the hot cup of tea John's wife had made me. We sat talking about the oddity of living in a house that has been assigned to you because of your contract with the church – the idea still baffles me. It was a very nice house in actual fact and had a delightful shower to complete the perfect package. I did not expect a shower but jumped at the chance when I was offered it. When you are walking nonstop all day, and smell like an elephant has shat you out, politeness goes out of the window and you leap at any opportunity to wash or to receive a proper meal. It is also, of course, a service to your hosts.

After receiving the delectable gift of pancakes covered in sugar, cream, lemon, chocolate spread and every other topping (it was Shrove Tuesday), I headed off into my minuscule tent for the night. I would be greeted by my camera goading me to ashamedly record a 'vlog', my pedometer informing me that one wrong turn had resulted in my walking twenty-five miles not twenty and my notepad tempting me to spill my psychological torments onto its speckle-covered pages. I slept with the uplifting words "Ope I don't collapse tomorrow' ingrained into my diary.

Sleep was the one thing that came surprisingly easily. Exhaustion created by a day's walking led to deep sleep so joyful that you could only wish for it at home. There was the occasional stirring outside, perhaps a fox sniffing at the unrecognisable material in front of them, though on this first evening probably the vicar's dog. But apart from that it was a sleep more comfortable than the many drink-aided ones I have experienced in a tent at Glastonbury. Bedtime was also slightly earlier than at Glastonbury; it would be 10pm at the latest. I did not attempt that night or any other to compound my exhaustion by staying up later; succumbing to it felt much more satisfactory.

However, there was the slight downside of having to wake up before 7am almost every day. Not the best feeling. At first, I said to myself that this would only be when I was wild camping because my camp would need to disintegrate into mid-air before the sunlight shone its torch on my whereabouts, enabling farmers to chase and shoot my skinny arse off their land. (I probably need to make clear that I don't think all farmers are trigger-happy people living in the Middle Ages. Only some.) Anyway, the actual reason I had to wake so early was because walking twenty miles took slightly longer than I had predicted, or Google Maps had predicted. I didn't wish to be walking late into the evening down country lanes in the pitch black and freezing cold, so waking up earlier seemed like a good solution to that problem. It wasn't. But that was all for later; at this point the challenge was just to reach Brighton. This seemed to me a kind of watershed before I would consider any implications for my future walks.

Setting off again in the morning from the Redhill vicarage I realised that it already felt like a week had passed since I had tentatively stepped out of my house the day before. Days feel like weeks when you are putting yourself through the self-subscribed torture of hiking with what feels like a donkey latched to your back. Day two would be easier, I told myself. I was now in the open, expansive countryside that I had dreamt of, with a network of footpaths and tiny roads leading me to Brighton. It *was* easier. It was mainly because I walked nineteen or perhaps twenty miles instead of the twenty-five I had done the day before. But the countryside helped. There are the occasional moments where you look at your surroundings and realise how much beauty surrounds you. Like the woods, on the outskirts of Crawley, where I decided to cook up a good old bag of Ainsley Harriot's cous cous. I sat, perched on a log, staring straight ahead at the deserted forest in front of me, admiring the grandeur of the trees soaring dozens of feet into the air above my head. 'Deserted' is, in fact, in large part a description of the entirety of my walks. The footpaths which my boots tramped were largely devoid of other human beings. Mainly due to the fact that it was February and the temperature struggled to get above 5°C let alone to double digits. The rest of the population had realised what I hadn't, that it isn't the most fun thing to walk in near-freezing temperatures. Anyway, I trotted away from the spot where I had devoured Ainsley's cous cous, and on to the river. Which I would then gracefully fall into.

And it was quite graceful, if I'm honest. I managed to limit the expletives to 'Fuck!' and 'Shit!', which I feel is pretty impressive when your feet are sodden to the point where every step is accompanied by a tantalising squelch. I had made the clever decision to ditch the footpath which had served me so well for the last couple of miles. On first look, it appeared to have actually paid off as I strode through the woods unopposed by obstacles. But then it became clear why neither that footpath nor any others had marched through the same route. A river. Well, I call it a river, but it was basically somewhere on the spectrum between a river and a stream. Not quite small enough to jump across but not quite big enough to justify the grand definition of 'river'.

I mean, I have quite strong opinions on the classification of rivers and streams, as if you couldn't tell…

So, on to the whimpering fool standing in wading-deep water, keeping the classification neutral so as not to offend. A plank of wood seemed to quieten my frustration. Well, at least until I saw it up close: the burgeoning algae in the rotten middle were not promising me a dream of triumphantly crossing the water. But with no other options, I decided to attempt the impossible: I would indeed try to cross the water in front of me with the aid of this plank of wood. It probably wasn't the greatest idea to carry my donkey-weighted backpack and camera bag on board for a mission which would surely impress the great Philippe Petit. I could feel Philippe's disappointment as the wood bowed to the pressure and quenched its long-held thirst, taking me with it. With the agility of Jason Bourne and the wit of Stephen Merchant I threw my camera bag up into the air and over to the safety of the bank in front of me, and probably looked more like a horse stuck in a hole than something from a James Bond sequence. I survived! The grand fifteen inches of water had not taken me along its current; I had warded off the strong forces of nature and survived!

You can probably tell such adventure and excitement weren't generally the main feature of my walks.

You'd think that with so much time to myself, I would enter stages of deep thought, resulting in a fully fledged life plan by the end. I didn't. I can't remember a single thought when looking back now, excluding the ones begging me to surrender. At no point did I have thoughts that would lead me to reconsider my life or provide me with some sort of solution to all the problems I thought I faced. My head was mainly dominated by the next road I had to follow or the next meal I had to eat. The dreamy prospect of a fry-up, a veggie one at that, sitting in my belly was often the main thing on my mind. Yet it was rarely acted upon. I still believed that, even after the psychological torture of the first day, I shouldn't eat massive meals out of the fear that it would cause indigestion, creating an extra discomfort I could do without. I was wrong. A weird cycle seemed to have gripped me where my belly would groan with discomfort because of the lack of food that had entered it. This led to every bite of food being a struggle even though it was what I desperately needed. It sounds ridiculously stupid I know. But I would genuinely have to eat all my food with little nibbles and bites so as to not cause a rupture in my stomach where all the food I had just eaten would spurt out onto the ground in front of me. It would be a slow process to eat double the number of calories I normally do...

It was much harder than it sounds. I should have been having between 4,000 and 5,000 calories per day at least. On a normal day, I would probably relish the challenge. But when you're walking dozens of miles a day this is less appealing. Eating when doing exercise is a struggle on its own – I'm sure all you brave souls who have attempted such an ungodly thing as 'exercise' know this. Then imagine that you are doing constant exercise with just little breaks throughout the day. Then add to that equation the fact that you are supposed to eat double the amount you usually do because you are burning so many calories that it is essential to eat that much to keep healthy. Too much exercise is unhealthy?? Something I'd like to hear more often. Anyway, I'm hoping that you're seeing the reasons why having to eat so much more is in actual fact a challenge. I've also never been a fan of counting calories. It is one of my biggest fears in life to become engulfed in such a craze because it stands proudly alongside the idea of losing weight, an even bigger fear of mine. I'm thin, not because I eat a bag of lettuce for breakfast, lunch and dinner, but because my body is naturally trained to shit at least twice a day. Or in other words, I have a fast metabolism. I actually eat more than a lot of my friends.

I know: how pathetic is it to be moaning about having a fast metabolism when other people gain a stone from eating a biscuit? But I've got my reasons. My fear of losing weight then transfers to the main reason I do not wish to become a vegan. As an attender of many environmental actions, it is hard to not feel a sense of guilt at the fact that you eat dairy in all its glory. It is just the exclamation of 'I've lost so much weight since going vegan!' spouted by many vegans whom I personally know that scares me into opposition. It's great, if you *are* looking to lose weight. But when it's your biggest fear and it is advertised as one of the main benefits, it's not so great. All this is selfish and exaggerated by my own fears, but it is a fear that I cannot get rid of and one that I have my own ways of coping with, in which logic doesn't always feature. So, food was very much needed by the point at which the sky above me was turning black – this was because day was becoming night, not because of some weird sort of *The Day After Tomorrow* shit.

I now had an interesting challenge ahead: wild camping. The snow that was now falling around me certainly helped lift my spirits in preparation. I hadn't managed to make it to my target of Haywards Heath, but Brighton was now less than twenty miles away. I could see a forest on my map. This was my chance. A few houses sat as watchtowers across the road. I would seek the approval of the individuals residing inside. They kindly offered me their water but dashed my hopes of creating a habitat opposite with the prospect of gunfire: the locals would be out hunting during the night. So I wandered on hoping that a local farmer would offer me a few metres of their land to camp on. Get the charity part in there, I told myself. Surely no farmer could reject a wandering cold soul who was simply doing the morally right thing. I didn't actually feel cold but it's always good to use the elements to your advantage. After a couple more rejections and warnings of the barmy old locals shooting pheasants, I headed on, but the buildings began to disappear as I fled further away from Balcombe. The prospect of being shot at while also freezing to death didn't really appeal to me as I wandered the lightless country roads of Sussex. My mother called (formal, I know). She saved me from self-destruction by informing me of a B&B a mile up the road, which she would lovingly pay for. My food-deprived and exhausted self probably didn't sound so grateful over the phone but, believe me, I was, Mum.

I trudged on. Past the roadworks blocking the road my OS map had taken me down. 'Watch out for the holes' is always a reassuring warning from the locals. Luckily my head-torch could guide me across the wooden boards and away from what turned out to be quite large holes. We're talking several feet deep and several feet wide. Across the wooden maze I leapt to reach the grand destination of the B&B I would reside in for the night. Pleasantries exchanged; bags up the stairs; food surreptitiously cooked on my stove. I was all but ready to go to sleep. Oh and I took a soothing shower along the way to wash off the dirt from the river that had welcomed me with open arms. Was just a shame its open arms had been made of freezing water and mud. I began to shake. I couldn't stop. My body felt as if some devilish force had taken control of me to remind me that I had committed myself to something I couldn't do. Confused, I thought it couldn't be the cold because the heaters, provided to replace the broken heating system, appeared perfectly warm. Was it food? Couldn't be, I'd just eaten. Maybe it would go away once I'd digested. Or maybe it was sleep? Yep, that was it. I fell asleep for a while after failing miserably to record my vlog; it's not too easy to hold a steady shot when the rest of your body is violently shaking. I woke up an hour later feeling drowsy, but no longer vibrating, so I made a few calls, texted Stan (the friend I would be staying with in Brighton), recorded my vlog and collapsed into the sleep that would carry me through to the morning.

Bleary-eyed, I woke up confused: the sun seemed to have broken through the white walls of cloud which had encompassed my world for the past two days. The spitting from the sky above me would no longer have to be contested with. Smiling down on me was now a bright ball of light which could only be a promise of a better day. I had only fifteen miles left: easy. Well, parts of it would be easy. Let's focus on that as I've been quite the grumpy shite so far. Always good to switch up the mood. Frost-covered countryside does create an appreciation of the beautiful world that you reside in. The rolling hills covered in speckles of brightness tingling in the sunlight that beams down on them can only bring a sense of awe. Standing in a field, knowing that you have walked directly to that place. No other transport. Nothing. It not only gives you a sense of pride but also, at the risk of sounding pretentious, it gives you a sense of freedom.

I don't mean freedom in the falsified American sense. (To any American offended by this, please stop using the word as if it's your mating call. You're not free, you're just not. 'Leader of the free world' my arse. Your country, like everywhere else, is so dominated and controlled by money that the idea that it is somehow the bastion of 'freedom' is utter bullshit. If you do feel like you live in a country based on 'freedom', well done, you are probably white and have a fair amount of wealth behind your name.) I mean freedom in the sense that I wasn't really connected to anything. I had no responsibilities, nothing to do but wander the country I had inherited as my home. I can't really put it into words but there's something special about using walking as your only mode of transport, waddling along to your destination with every bit of human contact feeling cherished rather than brushed aside like it is in the hustle-bustle of London. The contrast with living in London all my life was probably the main reason it felt so different to be in the open countryside surrounded by friendly souls. I'd also like to now completely retract my use of the word 'freedom', as I have just realised even more fully the reasoning behind my hatred of it. It is meaningless. Try to define it to me and then attempt to justify the exclamations by every American artist at Glastonbury of how much they love 'freedom'. Fuck off, seriously. It is just a bullshit word used by bullshit people.

All that didn't sound too positive in the end... Oh well... Anyway, I now began to see the South Downs rising out of the distance – this was my rite of passage to Brighton. I would climb the wall of chalky-green in front of me; it would be my final challenge to conquer. It was a bloody steep challenge, but I began to find the rhythm I'd been searching for over the previous couple of days. Step by step I climbed with little stress apart from a slight shortness of breath. My reward: a stunning view over the miles of ground that I had just conquered. Although actually I took little notice of the view behind me, and focused on marching across the downs that lay between me and my goal. Looking across these hills, it's impossible not to be moved by the beauty around you. Hills as smooth as a baby's bum; horses standing in ownership of the land around them; trees rising against the sunset. You could spend a day here and not get bored by just staring and admiring the design of nature.

My feet seemed to have found some sort of inspiration from the setting around them as they turned up the heat. Then I saw it. Brighton. The edge of the city stood staring back at me. Tears began to arrive in quick succession. My arms rose into the air as I afforded myself a little jump of joy. I had done it! I had walked from London to Brighton! Fuck Edinburgh, I had walked from fucking London to fucking Brighton.

It's a unique experience jumping, screaming and crying with joy whilst standing on a hill with no humans in sight. Your screams of happiness are heard by no one but yourself. It leaves the concept of being self-conscious miles behind you with the last individual you saw. The screams and jumps can be as high as you want. No one will judge you because no one will see you. Of course I was then reminded by a stranger that 'you still got two or three miles to go'. My blister oozing out the pus that had filled it didn't exactly help. Burst blisters aren't the most appetising things, both in looks and the temporary agony they cause. I still hobbled on, however slowly. Seeing the arches of the raised railway towering above the road ahead raised my spirits. I was close. With a little break for some inspiration from my friend Flo, I climbed the steps to collapse into the hug of the concrete block in front of me (Brighton station). It was cold, but it was comforting. Almost as comforting as the sandwich that Stan provided me with on arrival at his house, which was definitely an improvement on the extremely average bagel I had purchased inside the cold concrete block. (You know those really shitty mediocre bagel shops? The ones that sell bagels as if they are a luxury product and try to do things to bagels that should never be done to bagels. A bagel does not need to be changed. It is a treasure trove of sweet delight. Just leave it alone you wanky hippity hop bagel twats... They'd probably call it something like a 'Bagel Bar'. Wankers). But yeah, Stan's sandwich. That was nice.

So was the bed that greeted me for the night. Relief; happiness; comfort; sadness; pride; relaxation; love. Every emotion was absorbed as I burrowed myself into the soft comforting pillow below me. Leaving said pillow became quite hard. I had descended into its open arms as Stan deserted his house to pick up a delectable treat from the shop. It was my new love. It held me like I'd never been held before. Wrapped in its arms, I did not want to leave. The door opened. Stan called out. A pile of duvets and pillows responded with a soft groan. Looking to his right, he would see no sign of a human. My eyes had become gently but firmly fixed upon the ceiling above me. Movement was not going to happen. Well, the fact that movement would really only have involved hobbling slowly across the room, with Stan's bemused flatmate looking on with a doubtful eye, made it even less inviting. I would stay in my cocoon, communicating occasionally to reassure Stan that I had indeed not dissolved into the bedding below. It was done. Brighton had been conquered. Visited was probably a more accurate description. Anyway, all that mattered was that I would no longer have to walk.

Well, for four days at least…

Folkestone

February 2016

Four days of rest is enough, right? Of co-u-u-u-r-se. Well, maybe not, but shh, I was only walking like fourteen miles on my first day, so… it would be fine. I needed to leave on the Tuesday anyway so that I would be done by the Friday/Saturday and therefore be home to go to the Arsenal game that weekend. Football always comes first of course. You might also be a bit confused by the fact that I support both Arsenal and Norwich. Before you scream at me and denounce me as a fake fan with some weird sense of indefensible disloyalty, let me explain. I became a football fan around the age of six or seven: my first memory was Arsenal winning the FA Cup in 2005, which would then proceed to haunt me and my beloved football club as we stumbled through the next nine trophy-less years. Arsenal, believe it or not, is actually my local club. I live within a fifteen-minute stroll of the Emirates. I know many of you would probably think that Norwich would be the club I had a personal connection with, and Arsenal the club I shamelessly supported in the pursuit of glory and I a so-called 'glory hunter'. In actual fact it's the opposite way round – well, I don't support Norwich because of the 'pursuit of glory', as that wouldn't exactly be logical. I support Norwich because at the tender age of seven I played with them on *Fifa 2004* (yes, this is true), and so began to follow them in the league. Interest turned into support and support turned into love. If you want to question my loyalty, go ahead. But have you trekked across the country to watch your club in League One, the third division, a couple of weeks after they lost 7–1 on the first day? Most likely not. Being a Norwich fan is probably the opposite of being a 'glory hunter'. It's more like, as someone once told me, 'self-prescribed torture'. Whether I was witnessing Norwich's 7–0 defeat at Man City or their rise under Paul

Lambert (never should have left, you twat) from League 1 to the Premier League in two seasons, I have definitely had a mixed bag of emotions supporting Norwich, but I will stick with the lads until the end. While Arsenal, as many of you may know, is another barrel of laughs, but there will be no giving up in our endless failed attempts at winning the league. We will fight and fail until the end.

Sorry for that if you're not the biggest football fan – I had to squeeze it in this book somewhere. So. I set off from Stratford with the gloriously ugly Westfield shopping centre looming behind me. Folkestone was the target. Why? It doesn't exactly brim with excitement, I know. But it is the home of the momentous Channel Tunnel. And as I was originally doing all of this in the name of trains it made sense to visit quite a significant monument in the rail transportation industry. I mean, we're speaking about some exciting shit right now. Sarcasm aside, I have always actually admired and wondered about the extreme mechanics of building a tunnel under the sea for such a distance. As a child I dreamt that the walls would be made of glass and that all the fishes of the world could be seen elegantly gliding past in the most magical experience in existence. You can imagine the drab, dimly lit tunnel I experienced in reality being very much a disappointment. But still, the ingenuity of building a tunnel underneath the weight of tonnes of water amazed me. I do understand that the tunnel was not built in the midst of the water with diver-builders dressed in flippers and scuba masks smacking stones together. I just like to imagine the collective effort and mechanical skill which went into creating this successful engineering feat.

Where do we go now? Let's rejoin me on my way to a delightfully deserted campsite. I wasn't feeling too bad, in all honesty. No problems: body felt fine. Doddling along I went, largely beside a pretty horrible motorway-like A road as I wended my way through the less attractive areas of suburban London, to the day's grand destination of Purfleet. (I had already got pretty used to the idea of being the only reason certain campsites were open in February, sitting in my minuscule tent in the midst of a vast open field which I can only imagine would be packed out in summer, when normal people camp. It wasn't really lonely, just a bit odd.) Anyway, back to waddling to Purfleet.

I'd stepped up my eating game so was feeling quite solid for now. Hard-boiled eggs (won't crack) and a block of cheese and bagels. Couldn't go wrong. Although the never-ending long-road phobia came back. As a football podcast discussed the idea of Leicester winning the league in my ear, I considered the idea of lying in the smooth green grass that surrounded me for the rest of the day. I wouldn't get to the campsite, but I would feel comforted by the green tide that would sweep me to sleep. I gave it a little go, for twenty minutes at least. It was something special. The gentle sunlight shining upon my face as I sleepily gazed across the landscape dotted by the occasional grazing horse, wandering cow or bleating sheep. I could enjoy the view with that rugged feeling that I deserved it; I had worked for it. I hadn't simply parked up and rolled out of my car. I had walked miles to be able to admire such a calm, comforting scene. Lying, basking in the sun as I sprayed my face with a stream of cold water to awaken the wandering soul within me. It was genuinely an angelic moment.

Shame I had to carry on. And carry on I did. It was only a few more miles now. I would stop off at the next greasy spoon that greeted me. Milkshakes! They had milkshakes! Yes! Life was good again. I have a gentle obsession with the mix of ice cream, milk and whatever delightful flavours you wish to add. Gentle may be a slight understatement: I am the maker of many a milkshake. (A blender will be the only household item I need at uni.) So this would be a treat I could not have dreamt of. The chocolatey, bubbly concoction in front of me would get me through. The stares of bewilderment from my fellow café goers as I entered looking like I should be halfway up a mountain, not half a mile away from the M25, didn't faze me. I was at home; I had the homely comfort of ice cream and milk spinning around my mouth before diving into the slide that would transform it into the necessary energy. Milkshaked up, I marched onwards.

A locked gate is not always the friendliest welcome to a campsite. Nor is giving out the wrong phone number on its website. So I climbed in. I would find my spot, have a bit of food and then decide what to do. I had the added advantage of time on my side: it was daylight and would be for a few more hours.

Having no internet has many advantages. You can wander innocently without the ability, and therefore the urge, to check what
(only slightly) appetising meals people have posted on Instagram (if
you didn't make it then why are you bloody posting it?). Facebook
becomes something to happily flip through when you get the chance,
not an endless scroll of boredom as you pass the post you've already
seen five times that day. (I'm not going to try to say something you
might relate to about Twitter. I can't. I don't know it. Technically, I
do exist in the sphere but only as a 2012 version of myself. No one
likes the 2012 version of themselves.) But I hope you can relate to
that other stuff about social media and it's not just *my* sad self who has
often been known to tap on an app to cure the fact that I have nothing to do. If you hadn't guessed, the reason for my internet sobriety
lay in my choice of phone: a good old Nokia brick. Days' worth of
battery, quality ringtones, an alarm and of course the beautiful *Snake*.
Is anything else ever needed? I could call, I could text and I could play
Snake. Who needs the bloody internet? Well, in reality, I kinda did.
A lack of internet does bring the slight disadvantage of being a bit
fucked when you take down an incorrect number from a website, so
are now left in the middle of the empty campsite with no contact with
the owner. This is when mums come into their A-game. A phone call
and a log in to my email later, and Brian was on his way. I need my
mum's internet. Not my own…

Brian was one of those people who loved to talk, not in an annoying way, but he just liked to chat in an accent which I couldn't quite
place. Chattering away about his old Scout days, the oddity of Wi-Fi
and new technologies we didn't understand. He, like most, was confused by the reasoning that had brought me to his field. Although he
managed to relate to my trip to Penzance through a quite ingenious
trip of his own from a few years back. He and a few other ex-Scout
leaders decided to take a pilgrimage to Penzance via the help of local
buses. You see, they were all over sixty-five, so, as you would, wanted
to take full advantage of the free bus travel that comes with such an
age. Off they went: taking local buses across the country; staying in
Scout campsites or barns; drinking and laughing along the way. Just
having a lovely time. It sounded like a dream, or even a possible film.

A group of men with a fair few years on their backs, I don't think it's necessary to call anyone elderly, travelling across the country via the luxury transport of the local 22 bus having a ball of a time. When I retire, that's my new dream. Forget flying halfway across the world for a bit of sun, I'm gonna jump on a free bus and go wherever it takes me whether it's Penzance, Glasgow or Abergavenny. If there was one thing I could take from my heart to heart with Brian, it was that he knew how to live life.

With Brian back in his truck, I was again alone as I settled down with my tent. The campsite was quite cute. I could imagine camping here in summer being actually enjoyable. You could choose between the big open green expanse or a little wooded area as your tent-pitching options. I chose the trees – always choose the trees. Warmth, again, was sadly missing, so the toilets seemed like a slightly warmer place to cook up a nice bag of Uncle Ben's Mexican Fried Rice – best one of the lot, if you're interested.

With the Mexicans about to be down my throat, I began to mentally destabilise. Crying and cooking are never the best combination. Sloppily sobbing and stirring Uncle Ben's on a miniature gas stove in a campsite toilet will always be one of the lowest points in my life. Again, I had no idea why tears were flowing from my eyes, yet I could not stop these destructive waves of water. Exhaustion does weird things to you. Having no control of your emotions is one of them. So, as I hobbled back to my tent, I thought of a new plan which would, hopefully, not cause me to have continuous psychological breakdowns over the next six months. I would finish Folkestone but would then cut down to ten to fifteen miles a day instead of the disgusting figure of twenty. This would mean that I would only do the more scenic parts of each journey before doing the London to Penzance and London to Edinburgh walks in all their glory. Exhaustion-induced shaking would therefore never have to be experienced again. I would also be able to take more breaks, enjoy the country and just have a generally good time. I would no longer have to constantly worry about taking a twenty-minute break because of the ingrained fear that I would not reach my intended target before nightfall. Now I would arrive at my destination by 3pm with a few hours of sunlight to bask in, even if it was 2°C winter sunlight. I felt confident that this was the new plan to enjoy the next six months of my life and so, naturally, got into a ball of happiness and drifted away into the darkness.

'Left, right, left, right, left, right…' I had been bewildered as to why Sam had wished to instruct his feet on how to walk on our adventure to Epping Forest back in January. I mean surely his feet didn't need to be told how to walk; they'd been doing the activity for the past nineteen-odd years of his life. I hadn't noticed any occasion where his left foot had suddenly taken two steps in a row like a vibrating camel to rebel against its master. But now, as time went on and miles went by, I began to sympathise with the reasoning behind his odd behaviour. Rhythm. It was essential. I would convince myself that walking with a slight crouch would make my back ache whilst walking with a straight shape would cause the disintegration of my feet. I needed to keep to a certain rhythm. I would never speak it out loud like Sam. But I would think about it for minutes on end at the start of every day before drifting off into the daze that would carry me through the rest. Sometimes it would mean walking in such a way that I wouldn't notice the pain that my actions were causing. Sometimes it would just mean a way to push the pain from one part of my body onto another. It was largely psychological, but most things are. That doesn't mean they're any less important to you; it doesn't mean that it feels any less legitimate or real. If I could comfort myself with the idea that walking on one leg while the other dragged my bag along the floor behind would help then I would. If it makes you feel slightly more confident or happier then what's the harm in doing it?

'Get a good breakfast.' My mum's words stayed in my head as, on the second morning of the trip, I finally stumbled upon the café that would both save and doom me. 'Cheese omelette, beans and chips.' I wish I could accurately describe the feeling provided when devouring such a combination of foods but I can't. I can't do justice to the true deliciousness of this basic but beautiful dish (dish feels a bit fancy for greasy spoon food but you get it). Indigestion. It came as abruptly as that. Bellyaches had rocked my body over previous days because of a lack of food but now they rocked my body because I had filled up my empty stomach. I didn't take a break after. Key mistake. I was still on the twenty miles-a-day schedule, so any hesitation or pause needed to be humanely put down. I let Ant and Dec talk away in my headphones about their inseparable relationship, both publicly and privately, to help distract from the explosions within my belly. Eventually the uncomfortable feeling would go away to be replaced by a mellow feeling of food being correctly processed and placed. Sitting, well, lying, on the side of the road, I bemusedly watched a man in a horse-drawn cart roll up to the traffic lights beside me, wait patiently for his green light, and amble on with his day. Oddly, that wouldn't be the only time I saw a horse-drawn cart on my travels. Apparently, their extinction wasn't spelt out by the invention of cars and they still exist prominently across the British countryside. Cool.

My next hurdle would now be the grand challenge of crossing the River Thames on a local ferry. It didn't seem too complicated a challenge and the idea of being able to sit down for the ten-minute duration of the voyage appealed to me greatly. How wrong I would be.

Walking past weirdly placed tragic murals of musicians and their lyrics (Frank Sinatra's 'I Did it My Way' an example), I arrived at what was basically a car park floating on a river with a garden shed plonked on top. The garden shed was for the few poor souls, like me, who had not driven to this rather distinctive location. Little did I know that this hut would be my home for the next few hours. I was greeted with an old classic of: 'You better set up camp here, son.' Confused, I asked for the premise behind such a joke. The boat had broken down. Great. 'It happens quite a lot,' said the other half of what appeared to be a double act. A double act with the combined experience of at least 150 years behind them. The double act then became a cheeky trio. Then an awesome foursome. A famous five. Soon the shed was filled with a group of old codgers chuckling away about how 'Craig hadn't been seen out the house since Dave took the piss out of him last week'; Dave replied with the predictable 'Sandra's probably not letting him out the house', to which the shed erupted in laughter. They all seemed perfectly happy waiting out their days in this hut with little worry about the clear lack of boat to get them across the river. It felt a bit like an endless daily routine. Drive up to the port, stumble out of the car and plonk down for the day. Forget pubs, it was all about the little wooden hut floating on the Thames. Not so much for me. While the first hour passed, I sat considering my options as one of them proceeded to hand out tea to everyone. I'm still baffled by that. How one of them had enough tea for over ten people in his bag is beyond me. It was at this point that I realised a café would probably be erected sooner than this boat would be fixed. I asked the middle-aged cyclist next to me what his plan was but he seemed too engrossed in his own attempts to join the lads' banter beside us. 'Sixty-eight? Fuckin' hell, you were fuckin' born yesterday mate!' As entertaining as the group of ten seventy-something-year-old men was, I did have an aim for the day: to walk another twelve miles. So, with each joke cracked, I lost another few precious minutes of walking time.

It turned out that I would have to take the train all the way back to London in order to get a mile across the river – the British transportation system really puzzles me sometimes. My options were: go to the train station, jump on a train back to London and get one back out across the river to Gravesend; go to the train station, jump on a train back to London and go home for at least the night; wait it out in the hope that this ferry turned up before nightfall; or take a long-winded set of buses which probably wouldn't arrive on the other side of the river until nightfall. Great set of options there. I decided that I'd take the train back to London. I hadn't decided whether to go back out to Gravesend or not but after waiting three hours I just had to make a move. I said goodbye to the group of lads and the other inhabitants, chucked my bag on my back and trudged off to the local station. After an intense feeling of guilt about what seemed like giving up, I got on the train back, and decided to head home for the night and attempt to return in a few days. The reasoning I gave myself was the fact that it would be almost dark by the time I got back out to Gravesend – this was a fact, but a true adventurer wouldn't have let that stop him. You're either thinking right now that I was being pathetic or that it was fair enough to head home. To the first point, yes I was. To the second point, as much as people told me this it didn't make me feel better. It was giving up. I had let the small obstacle, well maybe slightly large obstacle, of a broken-down ferry get in the way. The day before I had been confidently striding along believing in the dreamy idea that this would be so much nicer than the Brighton walk, yet here I was sitting on a train home the next day. But I wouldn't give up. I would keep in my mind that group of elderly men who were so stoically resigned to the long wait for the ferry as inspiration to keep going. I get that that sounds like a strange type of inspiration but I derive my inspiration from a fair few weird places. More importantly though, I would be back... after the Arsenal game.

I now had a few days to sort out my new schedule, a more pleasant and slightly more sanely planned one. After much hesitation, I decided to catch the train to Rochester (little bit further along) not Gravesend on the Sunday morning (I took a little convincing from my parents). This would allow me to follow the new plan of between ten and fifteen miles a day. Off I set, and arrived in the city that was not. Looking upon the gigantic cathedral at its epicentre, you would reasonably assume that Rochester, despite its smallness, justified the definition of a city. Cathedral equals city is my usual highly elaborate methodology. Back in 1997, I would have been correct in my assumption. However, in 1998 Rochester lost the city status that it had held since 1211 (at the same time as Brighton became a city, so clearly the cathedral thing didn't apply any more), although no one actually noticed until four years later in 2002 – shows how much these things actually matter... Of all things, an admin error was responsible. When Medway, the local government district, became a unitary authority, Rochester-upon-Medway was absorbed into it and in order to protect its city status they needed to appoint charter trustees. And guess what? They didn't. Scandalous. Apparently they didn't realise it was necessary. So to this day, Rochester, despite many letters begging the Queen to give its status back, can only call itself a historic city. Even with that big boy cathedral sticking out of it...

Away from all these city shenanigans, it would be a good day of walking. I mean, I got to visit the actual Rochester Castle after which my local drinking hole was named. Although slightly underwhelming, the towering twelfth-century stone tower that stood staring back at me was clearly embedded in much more history than the Wetherspoons that I so often spent my time in. Well, that depends on what sort of history you prefer. If many a memory of stumbling, singing and shouting your drunken lungs out tickles your fancy more than a thirteenth-century battle then I'd head to the Roch for your historical awakening. Couldn't deny it was an impressive building though, even as Lycra-clad cyclists circled it in some weird sort of middle-aged mingling session. You rarely consider the fact that people who hung out with kings such as John or Henry III lived in these places. People who have lived lives so different from those of more ordinary beings that you can only consider their existence in fantasies or fairy tales. That is what intrigues me most, not the fancy-smancy castles or the dramatisation of Henry VIII's sex life; it is the idea of living a life of unquestioned luxury. Of course, luxury in a chilly stone castle with possible siege and every disease or infection under the sun likely to strike at any time is a slightly different kind of luxury from the luxury we witness in the twenty-first century. But my thoughts of course drift to now. It is not so much disgust or horror that crosses my mind at the idea of the ridiculous level of unequally shared wealth; it's actually sympathy for people who will never have the opportunity to live a more ordinary life surrounded by ordinary people who are not dressed up in ridiculous fancy frocks. They will never understand anything other than privilege. I'd also like to clearly state that I know I am fairly privileged myself: I have lived in the middle-class utopia of Stoke Newington all my life. So I am not attempting to claim I have endured any serious discomfort in monetary terms (I'm not a student just yet), which makes me incredibly lucky and I know that. But I'm guessing you understand my point about the royal family and their exclusion from the rest of society; this also stands for the Old Etonians who run the country at the minute.

After musing on the royals I toured the local attractions. A prison, the first-ever borstal and a young offenders' centre. Jolly hour that was. They were all weirdly placed along this long road up a deserted hill, far from the town, as if to literally represent the inmates as outcasts of society. Spitting rain and a howling wind didn't exactly help my fears as I walked along the never-ending, eerily empty road beside the ever-rising green fence which separated me from the demonised people on the other side. The size and hidden nature of these buildings was what shocked me. Walking through Rochester, you would never predict that these ugly and gigantic monuments lay at the edge of the town. I get the whole deterrent thing of making the buildings uninviting, forbidding, horrible, but surely being locked up in one place without being able to leave for years on end seems like punishment enough. They're going to get enough psychological problems from being in prison itself. Do you need to guarantee the whole thing is even more depressing by making the buildings look like the shittiest of shitholes? I think I'm going to lay off another rant for today – about how the prison system should focus on rehabilitation not punishment – as I've already punished you enough, think that's a good use of punished there (Oi Oi). For one moment I did believe that I could have stumbled onto an island, far, far away from the rest of British civilisation, and only inhabited by prisoners incarcerated in darkened rotting concrete blocks.

Onwards and downwards (I was now going downhill). Past a burnt-out car, across a fair few motorways and onto the Pilgrims' Way. The Pilgrims' Way has a rather interesting history. It runs the length of the North Downs (long bugger) and the trackway it partly follows has been dated back to 600–450BC with murmurings of its existence since the Stone Age (old bugger). Originally, it was not in fact a way for the pilgrims. It was just your regular Joe's ancient trackway. But then came along Thomas Becket, that Archbishop of Canterbury who was murdered by Henry II's fellas in his own cathedral. You know the one. After his rather unpleasant death (I'm not taking sides), he was given a little old shrine in Canterbury and it soon became quite the popular attraction. Christian pilgrims began to descend from far and wide. Winchester, a common meeting point for travellers congregating from the seaports on the south coast, became the starting point of said pilgrimage. The ancient trackway just so happened to quite nicely fit the route from Winchester to Canterbury, so a lot of keen Christians wandered down it to get to their old boy's shrine. Because of all this, it then became one of several 'pilgrims' ways' for a couple of centuries. However, and brace yourselves for this, the road I was on was not the same ancient trackway. It was the fantasy of a slightly deluded, yet enthusiastic, Ordnance Survey surveyor called Edward Renouard James, who created the 'Pilgrims' Way' in the nineteenth century more out of a sense of romance than in the name of historical accuracy. Meh, let's ignore that and act like I was walking along something that had existed since the Stone Age.

I would not leave the (half-imaginary) way of the pilgrims for the next two days – not a negative, by the way (for once). I began to really enjoy the beauty around me: the hills of the North Downs rising beside me on my left and the broad, flat farmlands of Kent on my right. It was great! I had the music, I had the views and I didn't feel like shit! I was happy. Maybe this was when things would change. That little glimmer of hope that had appeared a few days ago might have been onto something. I wished with all my heart that it was. I glided across the hills dancing away to a bit of 'Beggin' or 'Rock Your Body'. Life felt good. Occasionally, I would even spot another member of our species. We would glance at one another before politely nodding and going our separate ways. You see, the fact that I wore headphones largely expunged the possibility of actual conversation, leaving me plodding and dancing along, the dancing only occurring when people had disappeared from sight of course. The aptly chosen 'First' guided me down the final straight to my B&B for the night at the wonderfully early time of 2.30pm. Man City v Chelsea was on the TV. Fuckin' hell. Did someone give me a silver platter or what? Then my dad turns up to say hello and brings with him the money to order a pizza. He'd gone for a little cycle in the reasonably near countryside (completely coincidental I promise) – he was probably one of the many middle-aged, Lycra-clad men I'd seen throughout the day (it was a Sunday) – so thought he might as well pop in for a little bit of pizza and US politics on the TV. Sanders had a chance at that point (sad) but he did bloody damn decent from where he started anyway (happier). I have chosen here to inform you of my emotions through the useful punctuation that is brackets. I'm not exactly the number one person when it comes to grammar so I am currently debating in my mind whether the interchangeability with which I use commas and brackets is right, probably not (confused).

I'm gonna stop, I promise (lying). With that failure to inhabit the brackets with an emotion I will truly give up on bracketed emotions – sounds like some sort of psychological theory. The next day. Let's get back to the pilgrims and their way. Rain. It's not very nice. Once it starts it doesn't really like to stop. The H_2O dripping from my backpack adds weight and just a whole bunch of fun to the journey (sarcasm, I'm sorry). Still, it makes for good pictures. The haze in the distance creates an intrigue about what is hidden behind the clouds of rain while providing a unique sense of beauty by blurring the landscape that sits within sight. The expected dip in emotions that I thought the rain would induce never truly occurred; much as it isn't the most agreeable thing in the world, I didn't really mind. My waterproofs had it covered. Pelting rain was met with the strong resistance of Quechua and Karrimor's finest waterproofs. They had matched the bastard, shown the fucker: your water could not reach me through the protective layer of plastics whose science I didn't quite understand – or through the roof of the abandoned farmhouse I sat in for a nice lunch of bagel and cheese. Yes, bagel and cheese. Not cheese bagel. Bagel and cheese. Take the bagel, take the cheese, eat the bagel, then eat the cheese. Sorted. Then a lorry came along and I found out the farmhouse wasn't really abandoned; it just looked a bit shit.

Off I trotted with God doing the lovely thing of coordinating the end of his piss with my time to camp down. My chosen campsite was at another farm. Unfortunately, the barn of sheep next to my tent didn't manage to coordinate the stopping of their chorus of 'baas' with my arrival. That achievement was only reached by about 8pm, lasting until I cleverly alarmed the guard dogs into vicious barks, which woke the dozing sheep up again. They greeted me with more delightfully noisy yelps of enjoyment. You can't really get pissed at sheep; as much as the noises destroyed my sanity, I imagined the hilarious spectacle of these balls of fluff tripping over one another as they stumbled about looking for some sort of space. Sheep are just nice. They're like that one friend who can never really piss you off despite being incredibly annoying at times.

Barking dogs in the darkness, however, are slightly less innocent. I emerged out of my tent into the pitch-black surroundings. This, coupled with my genuinely awful vision, meant that all I could see was a general shade of – black. When that general shade of black starts barking, it doesn't feel too good. I paused as I saw the dogs disappear from the light of the barn into the dark that encompassed me. The barks grew closer. More aggressive. Fear that they would suddenly jump up and drag me away into that darkness took over. I stood still, waiting for them to calm or just leave me the hell alone. I'd be fine if I could see their faces and note that despite the aggressiveness of their barks they were relatively harmless. But I couldn't.

I'm assuming you've guessed how bad my vision is now. Let's just say I basically only see out of a single eye... and that one's still shit. After I spent a bloody long time playing chicken with the rabid creatures, their owners finally emerged from the barn and called them over. I took my opportunity, briefly said, 'Thanks,' and briskly walked to the poo pot. In fear of repeating the cycle on the way back, I sprinted and dove straight into the tent with the renewed hum of awoken sheep filling the night air. How could I be that shit-scared of a couple of dogs? I know it's a bit pathetic; I'm not usually scared of dogs past the occasional on-edge-ness when they bark a bit aggressively. But dogs and darkness together, bloody hell, that's not a nice combination. All I wanted to do was take a shit and brush my teeth in peace! Anyway, aside from the choir next door, it was a bloody decent campsite if I'm honest. Eggs, stoves, even packs of noodles were provided in what was luxurious living to me. You do appreciate simple things much more when you're just walking and camping about. Eggs, for example, are a unique luxury item because their crackability means that their existence in your pack would be a difficult challenge to say the least, especially as I flung the bastard off my back every time I gave myself a small second to breathe during the minutes I call breaks. All in all, sheep and dogs aside, it was a joyful last night on the road.

One more day. After an emotional goodbye to the way of the pilgrims, I was set on my way to rejoin the humans who exist within the great abyss of towns and cities. Ashford, that station on the Eurostar line which no one really notices or has heard of, would be the first of many centres of civilisation to greet me. Well, the bewildered teenagers in their school uniforms or the yoga'd-up yummy mummies didn't exactly give the friendliest hello, but they still looked at me and I hadn't been looked at for a while. Past the stares of strangers I strode on, with my imagination blooming with ideas of what sort of stories they were picturing in their heads to explain the limping muddy man strolling past. Most of them would probably come to the conclusion that I had a lack of sanity or justified the description of 'a weirdo'. I could pretend to be a man who has been lost in the wilderness for years, pretty hard in the UK with every plot of land taken up by a collection of tarmac, concrete and middle-aged men. Or a soldier on a training mission to scour the countryside for enemy troops. The believability of that one is probably even lower. My fantasies drifted on throughout the day, passing the time as I crept past town after town, village after village. With the number of miles left able to be counted on one hand, I sat inbetween a motorway and a train track. It doesn't sound beautiful, but the sights that surrounded me were. Hopping bunnies, gently flowing water and a delightfully sunny day all combined to create the most picturesque of scenes.

Unfortunately, I had to carry on. The temptingly delicate scene begged me to stay, yet the prospect of arriving home in time for Arsenal v Barcelona dragged me onwards to the nearby finish line. Of course, after a day of relative comfort, my body decided to kick me in the gut and open up the wounds within my weakened ankles for the final few miles. What a beautiful body I do have, always making things easy. Hobbling on along the waterlogged footpaths, I reached a weird smoothly tarmacked path right beside the railway. It didn't feel like a path that I or anyone was supposed to be on: you could literally feel the gushes of wind summoned up by passing trains a few metres away – surely it was just for workers? After a couple of peaceful minutes strolling, I noticed something a bit strange – a man was slowly clambering down a grassy slope that connected the path I was on to the bridge above it. It wouldn't have been *my* choice of descent but you know, each to their own. Less a smooth abseil, more a cluttered stumbling. Eventually, he made it to the bottom of the litter-strewn slope. He began to walk in my direction. Shit. Slightly perturbed, I minded my own business, right now not particularly wanting to interact with a human, and walked on. I wasn't to be so lucky. He definitely wanted to interact with another human.

'Do you know where Westenhanger station is?'

I did, and without asking why, kindly directed him down the exact route I had just taken away from the place. That was it. He wandered off to the German-sounding station and I wandered on to the Channel Tunnel, confused as to what had just occurred. Who was he? Why had he just dramatically stumbled down from the A road that lay above me? And why was he going to one of the smallest train stations I've ever seen? I had no answers and imagined what would probably be a much more dramatic tale than the truth.

I really should ask people questions in those situations... Oh well. I was tired, confused and not thinking about a book that I'd be writing in the distant future. I hope you can forgive me. It could've been the tiredness taking over, but I now began to witness the translation of road signs into French. The helpful reminder to our European counterparts to 'Drive on left' kicked them off (or 'Tenez la gauche' for certain recipients). It felt as if I had entered some sort of in-the-middle territory, international waters if you will... As if the little areas, in both England and France, which surround the Channel Tunnel entrances had become devoid of nationality and were stuck somewhere in between... That's all complete bullshit of course. All I'd seen was a couple of signs with French words on them, but I think that might give you a clue to the daze I had entered by my final day: romanticising every thought, every image I saw into having some sort of dreamy other-worldly meaning behind it. Now birds tweeting beside me were signalling their fear of the humans who had descended upon and destroyed the land that they lived in...

With the rolling hills of the North Downs bearing down on me from the side, I strode on with energy sweets rolling around in my belly to push me through that final bit. A sign! I was close – there was a sign talking of the direction the Channel Tunnel was in. I rounded the corner, recognising every bridge and blade of grass from the blessed Street View provided by the again wonderful Google Maps. Here it was, the dismal, depressing-looking workers' entrance to the Channel Tunnel. 'Workers' entrance?' I hear you ask. It's the closest the public can get to the actual Channel Tunnel without actually planning to go through it. Well, I could've jumped under a lorry but I didn't feel like the dyspraxia within me was very suited to such escapades. So I stood staring in from behind the rising gates. I had reached my goal but the adrenalin I had felt seconds earlier had disappeared to be replaced by the feeling of exhaustion and relief that I would not have to carry on walking. So I collapsed into the bus stop, waited an hour, and called Darcy and Flo before falling into the first of many forms of transport that would take me home to my much-needed bed.

Walking With a Mate: Norwich

March 2016

I think the main reason people thought I was insane was the fact that I was doing this alone. That would change this time. The Bavarian bear Sam would be joining me for my pilgrimage from Ipswich to Norwich. We would have a few weeks to plan and prepare for the journey that lay ahead, because the pain in my ankles had made me aware that some time off would probably not be the worst idea in the world. So I joined him in going through exactly the same stages that I had been through months earlier, with a little trip to Decathlon to stock up on both the most useful and most useless of hiking kit. Thick walking socks: necessary. First-aid kit: necessary. Safety whistle: less necessary as my lips could barely muster the kind of breath needed to awaken even the lightest of sleepers. Meaning that, if danger hit, the sound that would signal my distress would simply be the sound of a very flat whistle, not exactly something that screams 'HELP!' Of course there are many things that you should not go hiking without, but there are also many things that advertise themselves as these items but in actual fact are utterly useless. They are, in large part, a bunch of items seeking to deceive beginner hikers, like me, into buying things that we believe we need because of the very fact that we are beginners and haven't a clue what we are doing. So, basically, we're all pretty much buggered in knowing what to buy until we actually go hiking and therefore find out what is necessary and what is not.

Waterproofs. Aside from the obvious – trousers, shoes and coat – there are a few other waterproof thingies that did save not my life, but my dignity. Get a waterproof cover for your map. It's not helpful to have some sodden paper that's blended all into one to guide you from A to B. Without my little map holder for a mate I would probably still be lost in the middle of Sussex trying to spot where

Brighton was on the slowly dissolving piece of paper that lay droop-ing in my hands. Basically what I'm saying is maps don't deal with rain amazingly so get yourself a waterproof solution (I'm a bloody salesman right there). Buying the waterproof OS maps is an option, but a cheaper one if you're needing a fair few maps is to just buy a waterproof cover and stick 'em in there. I'm sounding all professional and that. I think you know that I'm really not. But I do know what helped and what definitely didn't. Waterproof shit helps. That's kinda basic but I very much learnt it the few times I brought my map out in the rain. Soggy blurry patches emerge. Just don't take it out, or find a good ol' tree for cover if you do. That sounds rather dodgy. I'm talk-ing about maps. Just maps. Let's move on. Dry bags. They're good and guess what, waterproof. If you don't know what they are… basi-cally just think waterproof bags which you can compactly pack and squish many things into. They work best if you press all that air out of them. It's quite hard to describe so Google them if I'm not clear. This then meant that my backpack was essentially just a bag full of dry bags with varying things in each one from clothes to cooking equipment (though it's a bit hard to press down on a pan and a stove). There were very few loose belongings. Basically, it's an extra protection for your stuff from the elements outside in case – no, when – your pack gets a tad wet. Sales pitches are now done, don't worry.

I mentioned the word pilgrimage in the first paragraph. I'm gonna give a little explanation as to why this walk was much more of a pil-grimage than the others. Whereas Brighton had clearly been a pil-grimage for a beautiful sandwich, walking from Ipswich to Norwich represented something much deeper. Football. As I have previously mentioned, I support the beloved Norwich City FC. Because of the grand emptiness of Norfolk, you have to travel from there into Suf-folk to reach the nearest football team, in the form of Ipswich Town FC (you see – they're only a town, we're a city!). So therefore Ipswich are Norwich's rivals: nearest club equals biggest rivals (how football works). So I would be crossing by foot the expanse of country of the Old Farm Derby to attempt to reach Carrow Road, Norwich's sta-dium, for the game on the coming Saturday. We would set off on the Monday with the comfort of beds for the first night in our heads.

I'd like to mention that by this point I kind of knew my ankle was fucked but decided to do the walk anyway – I think the word twat can be brought back again here. Well, I was just hobbling a bit before I started but the pain went away after a couple of miles; it was f-i-i-i-n-e. We descended into the wonderfully industrial Ipswich with the paparazzi (Sam's camera) following me. Oh, I forgot to mention that Sam's final project for his film foundation was me. For some reason people in his foundation class seemed fascinated with what I was doing. I mean, I know it was a *bit* odd. But not that interesting. I was basically just walking about with a camera and a fucking massive backpack. Although, to be fair, I feel like it could easily be interpreted as the pretentious wet dream of art students, finding your true meaning as you wander the British countryside staring out into the abyss that surrounds your own little human body. The emptiness of that statement surely deserves some credit for sounding so eloquent at the same time – I should definitely have been an art student. Maybe I actually am... But yeah, so Sam was following me with a big camera the whole way. Filming almost every moment, trying to gain emotional statements from me in my weakest ones (abusing your subject: a true filmmaker). Not gonna lie, I did have occasional episodes of wishing he would fuck off but the company was very much welcomed despite the slight drawback of a vast camera watching me the whole time.

Down the canal we strolled, into the countryside disturbingly inhabited by horses on chains. It was very odd: they each seemed to be chained to quite small circles of ground with no ability to move out of those circles or even communicate with or touch one another. If ever I could claim to have some sort of communicatory connection with an animal, my absolute sense of the pain and sadness in those animals was a good example of it. They were not a pretty sight. Neither was the 'Fuck ur mum 2k7' sprawled across one of the underpasses that we rested in. Even without my previous hesitations about Ipswich, it still didn't exactly appear to be the loveliest of places. I won't hold any judgement, though, as I'm sure there are plenty of beautiful areas in such a town, and in all fairness this was the surrounding countryside and not actually the town itself. So, onwards we marched towards the beds that we had arranged in Stowmarket, through a friend of my dad's. My confidence began to increase as my ankle did indeed seem to have stopped feeling any pain; I was a different person from the limping fool who had stumbled onto the train earlier that day. It's not always the greatest thing to be limping even before you've started. But all that really mattered was that I could walk and wasn't slowly falling apart bone by bone: always got my health as the number one priority. That almost definitely was my downfall.

You'd probably expect that walking with another human would be dominated by constant conversing – this is not the case. You may start off with a few words being exchanged on a regular basis but this slowly disappears as the hours pass. Communication becomes limited to the accepted directions of 'next left' or 'straight on'. It is no negative; it is a silence accepted by a mutual understanding of the toughness of what you are doing. You don't need to communicate because you both understand that you need to focus on one thing: walking without collapsing. Occasionally you might see a dead rabbit lying there and share a brief conversation about the disgusting nature of such a sight. All you need to know is that you can see one another and therefore know each of you is OK. We could talk at night; right now all that mattered was getting through the many miles left for the day. Occasionally Sam would attempt to break this barrier by asking questions for his film. I would usually shoot down the majority of them with rather pathetic answers, partly because I could not think of any other response, but mostly because I was devastatingly exhausted and barely had the capacity for my own thoughts, let alone opinions on other people's gap year plans. So it's no surprise that his film ended up including not a single word of direct conversation between us – though snippets of phone conversations with my mum and Flo managed to sneak in now and then.

As we stumbled silently down a main road, we decided to take a little break in a collection of trees to the right. So, with exhausted gusto, I threw my maps and camera bag to the floor (I'm still surprised my camera works despite the serious lack of care it is treated with). Sam then recoiled and calmly said, 'Gabey.' I turned to him, confused. He pointed directly back at the clump of leaves and mud I had placed my belongings on. A little face was sticking out. Not a human face. A snake's face. Those beady little black eyes surrounded by scales dotted with various tones of orange. I'm not the greatest colour expert so cannot think of a fancier Dulux-'look-book'-worthy name for it. Peeking out of the undergrowth, still as night (not too sure how night is still but, ya know). With a minute gone past, and no movement recorded, we came to the conclusion that it must be dead. Under this assumption, I grabbed my camera bag and decided to take advantage of the unfortunate death of the snake by photographing it (true photographer). However, as my camera snapped up a few shots, the back end of the snake, hidden under my maps, began to unwind. We then concluded, with slightly panicked exclamations of 'It's moving!', that maybe it wasn't dead. Sam, again the wildlife expert, decided to reassure me with the fact that it was almost definitely not harmful. So, with this knowledge, I decided to get a closer look and take a couple more cheeky photos of the bugger lying beneath me. Since it couldn't harm me, I selfishly disregarded its own wellbeing and attempted to get the best shot of a creature us Brits so rarely see. Anywhere else in the world and this would probably be a normal part of daily life but in the incredibly un-diverse wildlife of the UK the sight of a harmless grass snake would probably fascinate much of our population. So, by UK standards, I'd call it a pretty interesting day with the multiple severed rabbits and a surprisingly alive snake being served up.

Our residence for the night would be the unexpectedly accommodating 'shed' at the back of my dad's friend Paula's garden in Stowmarket. She spoke of how it was in fact Grandad's shed when he came to visit. This provided me and Sam with much entertainment. Just shove Grandad off to the back of the garden – can't come out. To be fair, I don't know if he'd want to come out… It was less of a shed and more of a mini bungalow with the layout of a room in a nice B&B. Tea, coffee, kettle, toilet, shower, beds and radiators. You name it, we had it. This was more like it. Grandad was living the life of luxury. After much thought I have decided that these walks would have been much more enjoyable if I'd had this sort of pleasure at the end of the day. As much as camping can be fun, after walking anything more than ten miles you want some sort of pleasure, not more pain from having to 'rough it' by sleeping in a tent. I realise that this probably sounds incredibly spoilt, given that a large number of people across the world have no choice as to whether to sleep rough every night of their lives: for them, it isn't a choice. It is their only way of life because they simply do not have the money or circumstances for any other standard of living. I understand that what I just said may sound extremely condescending to such people, and that what I am about to say may sound very insensitive, and I am sorry if that's the case; I am just trying to put my honest thoughts down on paper. I realised I desperately wanted a bed at the end of every day, and having to camp down and cook on a tiny gas cooker almost definitely lowered my morale. If I had known how much difference it would make, I would have tried to make a plan in which I could live in some sort of luxury or at least comfort for the majority of nights. Such as being able to sleep in a bed. Of course, a lack of money does create some problems in this area: there was no possibility that I could stay in B&Bs every night as I wandered around the UK. But, anyway. For this one night, we would be given the delight of beds and showers which we could truly relish. For no price at all.

But one small problem arose. My ankle. The deceitful feeling that everything was OK earlier in the day had been a myth. Walking had somehow become a painkiller. I could not feel the pain as I walked, further and further, but in the evening my ankle would seize up, rendering it intensely painful to move. Getting to the shower was a challenge, let alone the pub down the road. This was the one moment that Sam realised it wasn't just me moaning a hell of a lot. He could see the pain I was clearly suffering. Most people would probably treat my ankle injury as serious, but have not necessarily seen me in severe direct pain from it. Sam now had, and even he suggested that maybe I take a while off after this walk. This, coming from the most adventurous and full on of all my friends, opened my eyes to the stupidity that I had been living in. I couldn't just carry on walking as my ankles slowly disintegrated into the ground below them simply because I didn't want to cancel any more of my trips. My health was important, I think I'd forgotten that. I would attempt to reach Norwich without shattering the bones in my feet, and then I would take a month or so off. I had to treat my injury with the seriousness it probably needed. Diss then would be the middle point at which I would decide either to up sticks and give up because of the insurmountable pain or to carry on and bear through to complete my mission of reaching my adopted home town of Norwich. After all, this was only the first night.

Despite all this, we still managed to have a very enjoyable night in Stowmarket. Much of this we owed to the hospitality of Paula. The kindness of allowing two randomers to stay in your house was enough. She decided to double that by not only publicising my Just Giving page but also providing me with ice to comfort my fucked-up feet. So, thank you Paula. Thank you for being the most welcoming and kindest of hosts.

Now, on to another welcoming and incredibly kind host. Greggs. Fucking beautiful place. As a kid, I knew Greggs as the only place that would always have the iced delight I desired. My parents became fearful of this Beethoven of bakeries. The endless demands for a taste of the simplest, but most lovingly made, baked confection were ingrained into their minds. Basically, I liked iced buns. Quite a lot, and Greggs would be the place that benefited from this obsession. My automatic association between the two led to a fond feeling at the sight of those simply arranged orange squares that lasts to this day. The four mini squares make up a bigger bloody square: how can you not see the genius of this place? You're probably wondering why I've suddenly burst into a love song for Britain's largest bakery chain... Well, it could be the fact that it was the location in which we destroyed a gentle breakfast after breaking away from Paula's humble abode. More like Grandad's not-so-humble abode actually. This wasn't just your normal Greggs. It had sofas. Yeah. I'm talking leather. I'm not saying I approve of leather. I'm just stating a fact. And the fact is that Stowmarket's Greggs is fancy as fuck.

With intense comfort settling in my mind we set off for the day, out into the hazy distant sunshine, to continue our trek across Suffolk. I cannot recall the moment we crossed the all-important border between Suffolk and Norfolk so, sadly, if you have been waiting for such a moment then I cannot provide you with it. I apologise greatly for this awful sin. I can provide you with a description of the desolate town centre of Stowmarket though. Shall I go for it? Oh go on then... only because I can sense your intense anticipation. No offence to Stowmarketarians is intended (Stowies? Stowmartians? Stoweenas? I'm not sure what you call yourselves but – no offence to you anyway). This was my second visiting of Stowmarket and the town centre gave off a familiar devoid-of-life feeling. It was 9am. So, I mean, it's not the liveliest time in the world wherever you are. But, some life is usually evident. Walking down the High Street, decorated by closed, empty, run-down shops and unused benches, you'd have thought no one lived here (let alone 19,000 people). It felt a bit like a town of commuters who lived their lives in Ipswich or Norwich, rarely inhabiting their own town centre. Maybe I'm all wrong; maybe I should have come at the weekend when the streets would be busy and bursting with life. The thing is, I had been before, and they weren't. I just got this feeling of a depressingly bare town with not much going on. I might've just described half of the UK's towns... or maybe I'm just a privileged Londoner who's used to the overcrowded streets of the capital. Either way, it didn't feel like a happy place as we exited into the countryside.

After crossing the railway about ten times, we stumbled across a challenge I had faced once before: a stream. This one was definitely a stream, just to clear that one up. Easily jumpable, you may think. Brambled edges made our thinking slightly different. After deliberating and discussing tactics for a good ten to twenty minutes, we ashamedly watched as a truck calmly passed over said stream using the same road we had just left. All we had to do to cross was stick to the same bloody road... I'm not gonna try justifying. Let's just move on. Nothing happened. We smoothly rolled on into the peaceful village of Finningham at the surprisingly early time of 3pm. Food was on our minds. We would wait until the local pub started serving food at 5pm and then set off into the nearby woods to wild camp for the night. 'No food.' But there was a chippy van. Not too bad. My options were limited to the diverse range of chips and spring rolls; I had an Uncle Ben's to top up with later though, so life was all right. Jennifer, the pub's landlady, decided to engage us in conversation. She was, as any sane person would be, intrigued as to why two young guys had littered her pub with backpacks, cameras and muddy waterproofs. After hearing about our journeys and our plan to camp down the road, she revealed the day-saving fact that the pub had a little green patch which was sometimes used as a campsite (in summer, of course, because, again, that was when normal people decided to sleep in the wilderness). So we parted with our change and decided to get settled down for the night with the invite to the local acoustic night in the back of our minds.

Camping would be slightly different this time... Sam had convinced me to invest in the combination of a bivvy bag and a tarp as a lightweight alternative to my pretty shite tent. For those who are unaware what either of these two things are, a tarp is a tarpaulin to sleep under, which works by being tied to surrounding trees – or attached to walking poles, if the landscape is not so accommodating. A bivvy bag is then basically a waterproof casing for your sleeping bag, but more expensive versions can be high tech enough to fit multiple things inside, including your backpack, camera and much more. So put them together and you get a rain and wind cover along with a waterproof sleeping bag. The result is you can feel protected from the elements while also being able to appreciate your natural surroundings at the same time. Enough of the salesman pitch again; I'll describe my real life actual experience of such a combination. Sam had hyped it up to be this at-one-with-nature experience. I wouldn't exactly say that was an accurate description of my first night underneath a tarp, mainly because it was spent in a tiny field at the end of a pub's car park. Not exactly a naturalist's dream. But we'll get on to that later. First, we had the challenge of putting them up, and then attending the now infamous acoustic night, which we had many reservations about. Unfortunately, the area that would surround our camp was not especially accommodating, with a certain lack of trees, so we had to make do with walking poles. Walking poles, by the way, are utterly useless for walking unless you are tackling severe climbs or descents. Otherwise, if you're walking down a very flat canal path, say, they are about as useful to you as an overweight panda. So I was glad that I could finally put them to some sort of use in pathetically attempting to hold up my surprisingly large tarp. It's fair to say that I left our camp with a certain lack of confidence.

After about ten changes of position in the pub, we finally found our perfect seat in the corner. Jennifer's declaration that she sometimes 'joins in with her tambourine' didn't give us the highest expectations of the night that lay ahead. If you imagine an alternative sort of female 1980s rock singer with long curly hair and clothed in a baggy sleeveless top then you would arrive at an image not too dissimilar to Jennifer. Her rushed and dramatic conversations with her younger teenage fellow bartender added to a sense that she lived a topsy-turvy life with enough drama to fill many hours of conversation. We watched from our front row seats as one by one locals trawled in with their guitars, drums, harmonicas and accordions in hand. An awkward silence hung in the air at first, the gentle strumming of guitars being tuned filling the space as each musician, whether the teenage boy sitting next to us or the slightly older couple sitting in the corner, got ready for a night of gentle music. There were no microphones, no stage. We quickly realised that it would simply be a room full of local musicians strumming away on their guitars, soothingly singing along to the songs they could recognise. Without warning, it had started. The elderly couple suddenly opened up with the first song of the night. It definitely wasn't shit. Far from it. Our expectations suddenly jumped to a level we could not have imagined. As the music floated through the air, we sat, with our cameras, admiring the beauty we were witnessing. It was to be anything but the forgettable evening we had expected.

A seemingly deliberately mysterious man called Angie led the night with a sort of authority that he didn't appear to command. When I say 'deliberately mysterious', I mean as if he was *attempting* to be this mysterious character that clearly didn't come to him naturally, his hat partially hiding his face as if to symbolise how he is hiding himself away from the rest of society and all that bullshit (you know what I mean, or at least I'll act like you do). The others dotted around the room seemed to have worked this out many acoustic nights ago and there seemed to be an acceptance of this weird person who attempted to be the false leader of their clan. However, he wasn't the only mysterious character we met that night. First there was a man whose name I never caught plagued by a thousand stories. Whether about a girl he met in a waiting room or a lost lover from years ago, he had it all. Every song would be a story. He was a true performer. The voice that flowed from his mouth did not disappoint. He struggled to open his wandering eyes as he sang away into the night, with every emotion laid bare to the random assortment of individuals who surrounded him. Second came the aptly nicknamed 'Wild Guitar Picking Blue Eyes Johnson'. From first look, he appeared to simply be an elderly local who had wandered in with no part to play. My first thoughts were very wrong. Suddenly, he would burst into voice with no accompanying instruments. He would set the tone for others to join with the strums of their guitars. A voice that had seemingly seen a million places. A voice that would not speak, would only reveal itself in song. I aimed my camera directly at his face, attempting to reveal whatever lay beneath such an exterior. He revealed nothing. Just sat there, occasionally sipping his lager and placing a hat on his head for every song he took part in. A true mystery man.

A night I will probably not forget. Not only because of the night itself, but because of the circumstances we found it in. We had wandered into a random village pub and been met by a group of beautiful musicians whose offerings could rival those of an acoustic night in Central London. This from a village of barely more than thirty houses. Maybe some came from the next village along but, nevertheless, it was still a shock to find so many talented musicians in such an unpopulated area. This was what I had wanted to find when I set out to do these walks. Little encounters, completely unexpected, giving you a sense of happiness. I had been on the edge of giving up at this point but it spurred me on. I wanted more of this, more of these bemusingly beautiful experiences.

It was in my bivvy bag later that night that I realised I probably wouldn't have done that on my own: on my own, I had simply settled into my tent at night not wanting to socialise or see any other human beings, let alone visit a pub. Being with someone else makes you want to do more at night, makes you want to fill your time with activities and things to do while you're walking. It gives you the confidence to go and interact with others and to do things that you wouldn't be bothered to otherwise. Perhaps it could mean that I wouldn't succumb to the pain in my foot, to thinking I couldn't do something because it would hurt too much: I wouldn't care. There is no doubt that the shorter days in terms of miles also added to this generally more optimistic feeling; I didn't feel as much like I'd been sat on by an elephant, and I had more spare time. So, at that very moment, I was more grateful than ever that I had Sam with me along the way, and felt I wanted the same company for the duration of all my walks.

The night. It would be an interesting event. In many ways it convinced me that tarps maybe aren't the best way forward. We were warned in the pub of a rainstorm coming in during the night. Just a bit of rain, wouldn't be bad, we thought. Three hours later, we would very much disagree with our original conclusions. Rain and wind pelted our tarps leading to Sam's falling gracefully onto him and my face being greeted by water as I stuck it slightly out of my bivvy bag for the simple necessity of being able to breathe. So, as much as it kept the rest of my body bone dry, the bivvy bag completely failed to protect the part that's most important when you're talking about getting some sleep: the constant pelting of your face makes sleeping a struggle. Add to that the consistent rush of wind battering the same bit of you. I think it's fair to say it wasn't the most pleasant night of my life. The day could only get better, surely.

Nope. We woke to the comforting sound of more pelting rain accompanied by its best friend – a howling wind. So, after packing up what were now our delightfully wet packs and hauling them onto our backs, we took the only real option we had, which was to just carry on walking through the weather, the lack of surrounding trees or cover making it reasonably hard to do anything else. Then came the even greater news that we no longer had somewhere to stay that night because Jo, my dad's old friend who had been kind enough to offer us a room in her home for the night, had fallen ill so, with the idea of wild camping in soaking wet clothes and bags in the back of our minds, we desperately called my parents in the hope that they could create some sort of solution. They did. We were now booked into the Best Western right outside Diss, thus giving us some motivation to fight through the exhausting and demoralising weather that pummelled us.

We begged for some sort of protection from the heavy winds slapping us around the face, but were only handed long straight roads with little foliage in sight. I'm sure you're thinking I bet it wasn't that bad, or it must have definitely stopped later in the day. It didn't. Maybe for a couple of minutes along the way there would be the occasional break from the rain, but the wind was not so polite as to take the same time off. We just carried on trudging through field after field. The footpaths had become pretty impassable thanks to what I'd call a fair bit of flooding. I don't think I'll forget the image of me sitting silently in the prickly surroundings of a bush, attempting to protect myself from the cascading waters, while Sam sat a few metres away on a log staring vacantly ahead. Both of us were drained and fed up with being persistently dripped upon from above. Our only respite would come as we arrived in Diss, the rain beginning to slowly subside, along with its partner in crime the wind. Maybe the storm, which we had at first scoffed at, was finally disappearing. Anyway, we no longer cared. We'd reached our goal. We had made it to Diss, this being the point at which I would decide whether to give up or carry on. A decision which was about as important as the state of affairs in Panama to me at that moment. All I cared about was drying off, having a shower and sleeping until the sun came up the next day. With free coffees in hand, courtesy of the lovely station staff, we jumped in a cab to our beds for the night.

Suddenly the dream that Sam had been blabbering on about began to ring true. It was a spa hotel. A spa hotel! It had a jacuzzi. A jacuzzi! We had left hell and entered heaven. The soggy duo who had squelched into this plush hotel surely didn't deserve to stay in such a fancy establishment. Well, technically we had done the most typically 'Mummy and Daddy bought me this' thing in having our parents pay for the room because our own wallets could only dream of staying in a place like this. After a little confusion over the fact that my parents had booked the much cheaper option of staying on a Sunday two weeks away, we swapped the dates and looked forward to the moment when we would creep into our beds, intending to remain there for the fore-seeable future.

After transforming our bedroom into a drying room with the wet contents of our backpacks in a desperate attempt to make the follow-ing day slightly more pleasurable than this one, we discussed the idea of getting pizza delivered. Well, it wasn't much of a discussion. We wanted pizza, so we got pizza. (Pretty much sums up the conver-sation.) The evening would then consist of stuffing down said food before soothing our aching bodies in the luxurious jacuzzi provided. Our entry into the jacuzzi was a bit less smooth than you'd see in a James Bond movie. A grey mat sort of thing appeared to be cover-ing it. Was it closed? Our hearts sank. Please. Please don't let it be closed. We waddled our half-naked bodies round to reception. Upon our reaching the desk, the awkwardness of standing in a hotel recep-tion half naked began to dawn on us. Standing, waiting, I attempted to shuffle the towel across my body, hoping it would cover at least half a nipple. From the receptionist's point of view I probably looked like a pulsating penguin. Finally, the person in front of us in the queue was seen to. My bare, pale, nipply skin would only be seen for a few more seconds. It turned out the mysterious grey thing simply kept it warm so that our bodies could be lovingly engulfed by the gentle bubbly waters of the rounded tub. We scuttered away from reception, ripped the mat away and sank into the genteel surroundings.

It was nice. Very nice. No random bloke decided to join us. Always a bonus. If you've been in a leisure centre sauna or jacuzzi then you probably know the experience. A guy comes plodding along and plomps himself down next to you and your mate. Your previously utterly relaxed body tenses up as you are left in this awkward position of wanting to carry on your conversation while being hyper-aware of the stranger's body a metre or two away from yours. This didn't happen. Our utterly relaxed bodies stayed utterly relaxed. For the sec-ond time in the same week, life on the road (or on the footpaths, but that doesn't exactly sound as good) felt pretty decent, if I'm honest. Yes, all our stuff was soaking wet. But we were sitting in a jacuzzi with multiple functions, for goodness' sake! I mean, I feel like luxury is an understatement in this instance. We had gone from a state of being unwillingly soaking wet to a state of being very willingly soaking wet. A pretty good turn of events if you ask me. It felt deserved. It might not have been, as I'm sure many people did much harder things that day let alone throughout the year and didn't find themselves basking in a jacuzzi at the end of it all. But we were tired, low in morale and sodden beyond belief on what was probably one of the toughest days of my walks, so we needed something to lift our spirits for the final two days, and this was the perfect way to do it.

Weather matters. That's what that day showed me. Even more than distance. It may have been one of the shorter days I did on my journeys but it damn well felt like the hardest, simply because of the never-ending battering we had received. Distance may be gruelling – and long – but there are ways to keep your spirits up (like eating food, which you will remember I had smartly decided to barely do on my first day of the walks). However, when you're being pissed down upon and blown in every direction possible, it's very hard to feel even remotely sane. Without Sam I might have given up. Only the idea of both letting down his film and having to face everyone at home made me carry on. I wouldn't give up. It wasn't even my ankle which was stopping me now. It was the weather.

But what a pathetic excuse for giving up. What constituted that most everyday-British topic of conversation would bring me close to coming to a halt. After I had likely fucked over my ankle and carried on despite that. No. I could get through it. Walking might be very far from enjoyable when you are soaking wet and your pack is now doubly heavy because of its own sodden contents. But I wasn't going to stop simply because it wasn't enjoyable. If I'm honest, most of my walks weren't enjoyable, but I'd carried on despite my mental doubts, and I would carry on now. And yes, this meant that I was carrying on to Norwich.

Determined fucker. I'm not, by the way. I'm just a bit of a twat who is embarrassed to fail even if my dad preaches to hundreds on a regular basis about the need to embrace failure. This isn't in the sense of having a nice cuddle with it and then never leaving that embrace. It's in the sense of learning from failure – well, he'd probably ban the word 'failure' and replace it with 'mistakes'. Failure sounds too negative, you see. 'Learning from your mistakes' sounds much better than 'embracing failure'. I guess I could probably learn from the idea of not dwelling on *perceived* failure. We'll come to that later. I need to get to the point of *actual* failure first. It's taken me a while, I know, but we will get there. I promise. Up until then, you'll have to carry on listening to me witter on about my experiences of toddling around Norfolk. I think I'd passed into the wondrous county by this point just in case that was the most pressing concern for any of you avid Norfolkian fans. Also, is 'listen' the right word? Because you're not really listening to me, are you? I mean, maybe those of you who know me are imagining my majestic voice slowly read you to your death so are technically listening, or maybe this book becomes such a success that it turns into an audio book in which a random, strangely comforting actor reads it as if he is me. I have a slight feeling that the first scenario is more likely to be what happens. But if you are a stranger who is simply reading this book for pleasure (a concept that baffles me), then would you describe yourself as 'listening to me'? Or are you 'reading me'? Which sounds in many ways grammatically incorrect. Maybe I should get back to the entertainment that is my walking self...

Sorry for the slight diddle-daddle on this incredibly controversial subject. Hopefully I can steer away from it in case I do offend some of you. Let's focus on the sun. That was nice. I mean the sun is a jolly fella (or lass. Damn patriarchy). It's always bright and happy, looking down on us and the other planets which depend on its existence. Such happiness made its way into my heart. As I wandered through the vacant, slightly flooded fields with the beaming bright light of the sun behind me I realised that everything I saw around me was beautiful. Again, I had this sudden sense of why I was doing this. Why I had chosen to batter myself with rain and wind the previous day for no personal benefit. These little moments provided the answer. I felt happy and appreciative of the stunning countryside in a way that could never be replicated when it was seen from a car or a train. You have to be wandering down an unanticipated country road or footpath; you have to hear the distant tweet of a bird flying gently through the still air while the ground beneath your feet crackles and crunches as the tiny twigs are crushed by your unsympathetic boots. That was why. Appreciating the countryside that so many of us more privileged city children can take advantage of, while also having weird and wonderful experiences along the way, like the acoustic night on the Tuesday. That was why I was doing this. That was my personal gain. To create memories, ones that I really won't forget; to lock away beautiful, picturesque scenes with every dot on the landscape still apparent in my mind months later. These realisations suddenly flowed through my mind as I wandered away from Sam, into the distant sunlight that illuminated the winding roads that lay ahead. I was happy, very happy.

Again, Sam tried to pierce the protective shield that it has taken me years to create. Again, I would give him just about enough of an answer to be acceptable, yet not enough of one to merit a follow-up. Deflecting at its finest. This was not the time. I was happy, beaming even. I could not divulge the darkest moments of my life when the emotions that inhabited my body at that time were the polar opposite. I think every individual has his or her people. You probably have no clue what I mean there: let me attempt to coherently explain (it won't be coherent). You only feel comfortable in saying certain things to certain people. In guys, this is almost always someone from the opposite sex. Opening up to your guy mates, however close you are to them, feels like a quest impossible to conquer. It is as if being vulnerable in front of a fellow male makes you in some way less masculine, so, even though I am as close to many of my male friends as I am to my female friends, the only time I would ever 'open up' to them would be accidental, during an intoxicated rant. Whereas, even though I keep most of my mind locked away from human contact, I am comfortable in revealing certain clues about my inner demons to my female friends. It feels like a natural thing: when a guy and girl are best mates they are naturally trained to be more in tune with one another's emotions whereas there is no such natural training between male best mates. The basis could probably be found in some sort of ingrained idea of a stereotype: girls are in some way more caring than guys and so we are more likely to receive the response we wish for from our female friends. So that is why Sam will not hear about the pains of my life, especially with a camera pointed at my face. I am a friendly and open person but privacy is something I will not relinquish. (Ironic, this being said in a book basically about myself.) But I am in control of this book. I decide at which point to stop. I can hide what I need to hide.

Let's tiptoe away from my personal philosophical opinions on friendships back to the simpler world of walking. After a day of genuine peace, of strolling slowly along empty roads with the distant tree line standing tall at the edge of the painting that lay before us, we began to think about sleeping. I had marked on our map a tiny bit of forest, near Forncett St Peter, which appeared to provide some sort of cover for the night. It was en route so would cause no delay and would provide us with shelter if we were hit by another torturous storm.

As we sat, resting, on the side of a small country road, a local fellow and his dog greeted us with much energy. An energy we could not reciprocate, largely because of the previous four days, but also because it would genuinely be a challenge to reach those levels of energy, and of friendliness, that he offered. We talked about possible camping areas, from distant fields to mini forests, before he and his classic Norfolk accent wandered off. After a few minutes of us sitting silently appreciating the gentle nature of our surroundings, he returned. He now had more energy than before. He even did a little hop and a jog to join our party again. We were then provided with another option to compete with my teeny tiny forest. He owned a small piece of land just across the hill from our current whereabouts, no further than a ten-minute walk away, which we could sleep on if we wanted to. The neighbour was apparently 'a bit of a twat' but would clear off if we instructed him as to who had offered us the land. 'But the chap over the road is a nice chap' who would 'sort us out' if we wanted 'water or anything'. How lovely and friendly is that? Offering two random guys your land to camp on despite knowing next to nothing about them. A beautiful man with a beautiful accent.

We now had an important decision to make. Forest v Random Man's Land. We let the conversation run its course towards finalising such plans. The forest would win. Not because of any doubt we had about the man who had just graciously offered up his own private land, but because it was slightly out of the way and would mean our final day would be made longer. That was not what I wanted. I had reached the point where I needed that final day to be easy. I could do it; I just didn't want anything unnecessarily extra added on to put my ankle through more agony. So we wandered off to find the forest and finally indulge in the mysterious adventure of wild camping.

A couple of hours and a half permission from a local neighbour later, we were camped down and ready for the night. This was more like it. If camping under a tarp was always like this then I would appreciate it a hell of a lot more. Sitting out in the open, with the stars shining down from above and the gentle tweets of the birds getting ready for bed surrounding you, in a natural landscape we have become unnaturally separated from. I accept that it's been a fair few thousand years since the majority of the human population lived at one with nature but I don't think our natural destiny in this world was to build huge concrete blocks to hide us from that world we originally belonged to. So, another pretentious line... But I felt an actual sense of being in the wilderness, away from human civilisation (despite there being a house less than 200 metres away), because there was no distant hum of cars ploughing through the country stillness; there was silence. It was great!

The problem with tarps is that they're fine in this sort of weather but in an actual rainstorm it's very hard to not get wet at all. Hardcores would probably tell me that a little drip wouldn't hurt me. I don't care if it wouldn't hurt me. But the point is, it would most likely disturb me or the sleep that I had settled into. Again, I'm not doing this walk thing to rough it up or to feel like I've forced myself through some sort of pain to reach my destination. I'm doing it because I want to explore, and the luxury of a tent in a rainstorm is slightly more comforting than the open-air, largely unhelpful tarp. Sam would probably say that I'd done it wrong or we'd had one bad episode, but even his tarp had failed him despite his years of experience in this area: even he had got wet during that memorable night of the storm, so he cannot convince me that they offer better protection than we enjoyed. If the weather's going to be nice then yes, maybe I'll consider a tarp and a bivvy bag, but if there is any sort of uncertainty on the weather front then, sorry, I will have to stick to the good old reliable tent. Even if mine is shit.

I realise that my wanky talk of how humans should live within nature, not separated from it, is slightly hypocritical alongside my persistent talk of luxury and the comforting nature of B&Bs, but it's still an important point and I would support a move into nature if it came about. This wouldn't mean ditching our intelligence or technology; we could continue to develop these in the natural world, building our own communities within nature using that intelligence, and yes, that technology, to help us to become more self-sufficient. I know this sounds like an anarcho-syndicalist's wet dream, and it is very much 'a dream', but why shouldn't I dream? If you dream of something hugely ambitious, then, even if you achieve at least part of it, you end up with a situation better than what you started with. And that's progress. OK, I'm not an anarcho-syndicalist. I largely believe in still living in the way we do now, but powered by a cocktail of different renewable energies rather than the slightly less tasty cocktail of oil, gas and coal which we currently rely upon. So, although I do believe in the need to cut down on the demand we put on the world with unnecessary luxuries, I understand that separating off to live at one with the natural world is largely unrealistic because of how separated we have already become from it. 'Live within our means' is something the First World doesn't exactly understand. I'm not claiming to be some sort of innocent who has all the answers in this picture; I probably consume huge amounts more than anyone living in a less developed country simply by using what is provided for me. For example, I surrendered to the consumerist and capitalist culture surrounding us by getting chips and mozzarella sticks from McDonald's last Friday night without hesitation. Doesn't exactly sound like the biggest crime on earth, but in the process I am accepting the idea that we need these unnecessary commodities in our lives while also endorsing low wages, a poor environmental record and the mass production of meat. Of course, these are three things which I naturally oppose. But in nearly every walk of life we will endorse such things almost every day simply because of the world we live in. So I'm not perfect in any way; I just try my best while the way much of our world works is not perfect either. But the world definitely *doesn't* try its best, and that's all I'm asking for. Let's just try our best: commitments which will only limit the warming of the earth to 3°C are not trying our best – it's simply an attempt to look as if we are trying. We can do a hell of a lot better.

Tweeting birds woke us before 6am, reminding us that we were wild camping and needed to pack up as quickly as possible before full daylight. This is because wild camping means camping on some-one else's land, which in England is largely private land. We had been gifted with the knowledge that the owner of this little wood – I realised forest was much too fancy a description for what it was – resided in Norwich. With ten or so miles between us and that owner, we had confidence that we would probably be left undis-turbed. Despite this, precautions were still necessary. So the 6am wake-up call was still very much needed just in case of the slightest possibility that some angry screaming owners might come along. It's always a bit harder to claim that you haven't slept somewhere when you have a tarp and a sleeping bag out, as opposed to simply having a backpack resting against a tree. 'Oh, that backpack. Just giving it a nice old nap. Don't worry.'

There was a delicate frost complemented by a dashing of mist to greet us as we exited the woodland (changing it up). A morning dew sparkled on the grass. As we wandered, we passed dottings of eggs and apple juices sitting on tables outside farmhouses waiting to be bought by the locals or walkers. Walkers, oddly, seemed like the main tar-get; the supplies were often far from a road so customers could only have been expected to come via the old-fashioned mode of transport: using their own two feet. In our modern supermarket-focused world, I still find the existence of such things quite heartwarming, the local economy still pootling along. As well as the eggs and the juices, the morning really was stunning with the mist that gently hung in the air. Mist just makes everything a bit more mystical. Looking out onto the field in front of you, not knowing what lies on the other side because a layer of icy air stands in your way. Its mysterious blurring of the landscape gave the final morning an appropriately magical feeling as we stood upon a raised footpath, gazing over the tenderly obscured countryside.

In a hazy sunlight we marched through endless fields occasionally dotted by not-so-wild animals ranging from bulls to horses (we're in England; it was never going to be more exciting than that). The bulls were quite excited though. Maybe a bit too much... Jumping and chasing one another around the field as we looked on, commentating from behind the reassuring safety of a wooden fence. Eventually, they wandered over to us in that inquisitive fashion farm animals do. The slow wander, with a hint of caution. Sam's delightful welcome of 'You're gonna make juicy burgers, you are' justified their hesitation. The atmosphere got a bit awkward after that; leaving the bulls to ponder their mortality seemed like the best option. Bye-bye to the bulls, hello-hello to some ponies. Well, a whole sanctuary full of them in fact. Accidentally stumbling into such a location was rather nice. The backdrop to the fields that the ponies inhabited painted quite the beautiful picture: a row of trees in the distance, with a small wooden hut placed at the centre of the fairly muddy field that had been shaped by the hardened hooves of its inhabitants, and all of this covered and illuminated by a delicate haze providing the softness that only comes on a winter's morning. After a fair bit of stroking (of the ponies, not each other), we ambled on with that picture resting safely in the back of our minds.

The last day brings both excitement and a dreaded feeling that it is going so much slower than you wished. Every mile feels like five more, all the aches and pains from the past five days combine to leave you scraping to the finish line. Then it came! A sign that it was almost over. A literal sign, which proclaimed that Norwich was the grand total of 'four miles' away. I had done fifty-six and now I had four left. Four measly miles to fight through. For the first time since the inaugural day I placed headphones on my head. Music, not Sam, would be my main accompaniment to the fanciful final destination that was Norwich's finest Holiday Inn. This was no longer about appreciating my surroundings; it was about reaching the final destination with as little pain as possible. Long, slightly industrial roads would lead us into the more aesthetically pleasing centre of Norwich as Sam attempted to remember a voice that he had tormented me with days before.

I lied and claimed to remember how it went, then added to his frustrations with my refusal to reveal the sound. He muttered on, musing over the possibilities of what it could be as I walked ahead hoping he would not remember the devilish tones. Across a bridge, along a never-ending road, down a massive hill, across another bridge, and there it was. The beauty that is Carrow Road was in our sights. We stared in appreciation at the grandeur of what stood before us. I had experienced many fine games in that ground. I would experience a pretty pleasing one the next day (0–0 with Man City, not a bad result if you ask me). Then, with little hesitation, we fucked off to the Holiday Inn (it's in the corner of the ground in case you didn't know). Rest and the ability to appreciate that we had finished the fucking thing were of utmost importance.

Let me explain the Holiday Inn. My dad and I had decided to realise our dream of staying in one of the rooms that overlooked the pitch at Carrow Road. We had always whispered and wondered about how it worked: were people allowed in the rooms as the game was on? How good was the actual view of the pitch? To the first question, yes they were but only if staying the Saturday night (luckily, we wouldn't be missing out because we actually had tickets to the game). To the second question, pretty fucking good. Even better when you get to watch the sunset behind the stands being slowly replaced by floodlights that grandly illuminate your room, quite bad for the environment but quite nice to look at. It might sound sad to many of you non-football fans, but it felt pretty special to be where I was. It was also a pretty good shot for Sam's film. So yeah, Dad was on his way, just had to wait a few hours in this hotel room, what a torturous experience that would be... Sam's decision to join me in the room as I waited on my dad's arrival didn't bother me, at first. But then came the desire to be alone. The 'want to have a couple of hours to myself lying in a bath after five days of constant company'. This was not to bash Sam. We had survived five days with barely a bad word spoken to each other; walking sixty-odd miles in a fair amount of pain without an argument is pretty impressive. Ruining that

now, after we'd done it all, was not what I wanted. So, after a little impatient encouragement, Sam headed back home to London.
I would get a couple of hours to pamper myself. Lying sprawled
out across the comfort of a fine-arse bed, I felt a sense of fulfil-
ment come over me. We had done it! We had done exactly what
we set out to do. We had walked from Ipswich to Norwich and
I, despite the searing pain in my ankle, had largely enjoyed the
trip. Shame I wouldn't be able to walk like that again for a long
time...

A Load of Shit

Nowhere in Particular – March to May 2016

This is hard. Writing this. I just wanted to let you know that, before I indulge in describing the collapse of my year. A bit forward, I know. Not exactly holding many clues back. But it's finally time to confront this chapter. Here we go...

I have flat feet. That was it, that was the big deep and dark secret that I wished to face up to. Sarcasm. I won't put it in brackets this time. On with my feet. They're not the greatest things for walking. I didn't really know this. I found out that feel-good fact in my second session of physiotherapy. It was a shame the physio hadn't told me in the one before my walk to Norwich. Apparently she never expected to see me again because I appeared to be one of those people who kind of downplay injuries and don't believe they need any help from people like physiotherapists. This was true. I can't really deny it. My mum was the person who convinced me to go in the first place and then, after the often torturous pain throughout the Norwich walk, it was almost a form of self-harm to not go back. So, there I sat in the physiotherapist's room. I'm not going to lie... I did find her oddly attractive. But I shall not go into that for fear of sounding in some way sexist for focusing on a woman's looks and not her profession. And I was much more appreciative of the profession, as I did kind of need it at the time. We made the mutual decision to aim for a month in terms of being able to walk across the country again. This wasn't the worst thing in the world for me as after a month of being all over the place I quite enjoyed the idea of being able to chill out at home for a while. Apart from the fact that I was limping around for a couple of weeks, it all seemed OK. 'It should be back to full strength in six to eight weeks.' That did seem like a long time but not the worst thing in the world. 'We'll try to do it in a month,' she would half-confidently say as she pierced the skin of my legs with dry needles. I believed her.

I didn't really tell you what was wrong with my feet, did I? I'll just tell you about my vague understanding of it at the time. I had basically fucked up the area around my ankle and made it very inflamed; the other one was pretty fucked too but not as bad. Positive: no structural damage. Negative: I didn't really understand what was wrong with me. This is my main problem with doctors or people in the medical area. They don't speak English. They speak in some jumbo-flumbo language of technical-bullshit-medical words which no one bloody understands! You have to force them to speak in normal-person language to actually understand and even then it's a bloody hard effort. So, even though I later found out that she could've explained it in a much simpler and easier way, she decided to demonstrate what was wrong via the help of a plastic model of a foot. She appeared to be showing me something to do with a gap in between two parts of my feet being closer than it should be. If I've lost you, don't worry; I was very much lost in the hills at this point. All I could gather was that I had an 'ankle inflammation' from 'walking too much' because I had 'flat feet'. If you think this is an in-depth understanding of my problem then maybe I am a prat but I do not believe anyone effectively explained my problem to me. Even though I only understood about one word in every sentence, I still believed her. She was the medical expert in the room; what else could I do?

Away from that little room, my enjoyment of being back in London began to falter. At first it seemed enjoyable to just kick about basically doing nothing with my life. After a few days of being at home fixated on screens I began to feel bored and useless. I sat there, not knowing what to do. I was told to rest so my maximum activity could be going to the pub while others would go out clubbing. I wished I could join them. Dancing was the one thing that I longed to do. It provides me with happiness, and not being able to dance, and not being able to do so many other things – from any sort of sport to even walking for longer than twenty-five minutes – to have all that taken away just because I had 'walked too much' hurt me desperately. Norwich had made me want to carry on, not give up. But now it seemed like a distant memory that I wouldn't repeat for an unbearably long period of time. If I wasn't walking I wanted to at least be having fun. I wanted to be going out enjoying myself, not stuck at home on my laptop endlessly scrolling through the news or my Facebook time-line. I didn't want to be that guy who told his mates to slow down because he could only walk at half the pace of the average walker. In fact, I got so fed up of being that guy that I stopped asking. Attempting to walk as fast as many of my seemingly Usain Bolt-like friends probably made my feet worse. But I couldn't keep on complaining and moaning about the almost constant pain. I didn't want to be that guy. Anyway, it would all be better soon, so I wouldn't have to ask any longer. I would be able to go out and actually enjoy myself. Just a waiting game.

After a couple of weeks of swapping my feet from freezing cold to boiling hot water, having some more needles stuck in me and getting what I'd call a 'rough' massage of my calves, I was told of my perfect night at XOYO. If you've been out in North London, you've probably heard of or have been to XOYO. It's in the wonderfully gentrified Shoreditch (I want to make clear that that was sarcastic). A hipster's wet dream is maybe a more fitting description of the area. Drive the locals out but pretend to be social justice warriors and 'poor' while you sip your three-pound-a-cup artisan coffee and comfortably pay the £2,000-plus-per-month rent. They are wonderfully wanky creatures aren't they? Don't even get me started on Stoke Newington Church Street. Slight diversion... Back to XOYO. It's a club. Quite a decent one at that, depending on the club night as with most. The night in question would be a disco one that all my friends had committed themselves to going to. I sat nervously in my physio's room. With incredible tentativeness, I popped the question. 'Can I go?' There was an eerie pause. 'Next Thursday? Yeah, that should be OK. Just be careful.' I had permission! I could go out!!! I don't think you can process how happy this made me. I would be able to dance to disco, soul and funk until the early hours. I had been searching for such a night for the months before I fucked up my ankles. I would have to be extra careful for the next week and a half. Like the sort of careful where I would limit my walking for the next week while also making sure that I didn't attempt to bust the occasional cheeky dance in the kitchen. Day by day, I would assess the situation. Day by day, I began to disregard little aches and pains as nothing bad enough to stop me going; the desire to go back to normality clouded my judgement. I, and my physio, should've known better (a lot better).

It came, my big day. No, I wasn't getting married. I was going clubbing. Can I make a weird, sort of true, comparison about clubbing and weddings? I'll give it a go: the two are both often awkward at first while you talk or dance around many people you do not know with a confusion about what to do or say. But, as you ingest more alcohol, the awkwardness gradually disappears to the point where you end up dancing with a random group of strangers who are very much not your friends/family. This might just be my experience of clubbing mixed with my perceived view of what weddings are like for fully grown adults. Let me remind you that as I write this I am the tender age of eighteen (might be nineteen by the time this is completed, or even twenty...) so weddings are not exactly my forte. Think I did pretty well though to be honest. Let's head to a different part of my brain now: my memory. I should probably remember which part of the brain this is located in but my Psychology AS level didn't really stick in my mind. I wanted to drop that bugger from the moment I realised I wouldn't be analysing people's problems for the duration of the year. Now, let us actually go back to my much-awaited return to the clubbing world. I was ready, and a little dance in my kitchen to test out the ability of my feet to dance the night away was undertaken. The first few minutes appeared solid. A twitch. Just a little glitch? Let's ignore it. My hopes for the night were slightly lowered by this twinge of pain in my ankle, but I could overlook it. I wanted to have fun. Just to clear it up, I felt pain all the time in my ankles, but that was as in a little pinch of pain, while this was a sharp random shot of pain. It went away relatively quickly and I decided it would be OK. After all, my physio had said the same. What could go wrong? (Hope you like the perfectly cheesy paragraph ending.)

For all the negativity, up until this point I had been making slow and steady progress. I had the aim of walking from Settle to Carlisle in the next month. Eighty-odd miles. I could do it. I would tell every soul from my grandparents to distant friends that this would be my new schedule. Sometime in the first few weeks of April, I would be off again. Day by day it did feel as if it was getting slightly better even if I could still feel it in every step I took. The sensation of pain was partly because, as my mum never-endingly repeated, I was over-thinking it, but largely because the pain was also very much still there. But the excitement of getting back to normal life was rising, with the disco night at the heart of this. Off I went to my mate Maisie's house for the grand occasion of pre-drinks. An hour later alcohol would be sitting comfortably in my belly while the rest of my body dealt with the consequences. After a nice little session of singing football chants for the duration of the bus ride, with the added benefit of pissing off not only everyone we were going with but everyone who had the misfortune of sharing the bus with us, we were off and ready for the night ahead. It's not always the best thing if the bus driver flashes the top deck lights (translation: 'Shut the fuck up'). My weariness about my ankles still sat, tickling away, at the back of my mind as I made the decision to take my ankle brace off. It felt like it was restricting/ damaging me more than it was helping. I cannot tell you whether this was a good decision or not; I was slightly intoxicated in a club toi-let when I did it, so my mind wasn't exactly in the clearest place. It had started off well, albeit very drunkenly, my feet felt OK, and I had given myself the necessary regular breaks, consisting of sitting alone on ledges in the club.

Pain. It didn't take long. Settling into the edges of my ankles as I attempted to dance the night away. Emotions, intensely enhanced by my drunken state, began to take over. They weren't positive. I was watching all my friends dance with so much happiness and not a care in the world whilst I sat on the edge of the stage staring, wishing that I could do the same. I couldn't. Every time I stepped up to dance I knew that it was only making it worse. I sat, occasionally shuffling to the beat if one of my friends looked over as if to encourage me to get up and break out every move in the book. It wasn't a sense of devastation, more of disappointment. A general acceptance set into my brain as I adopted a Beyoncé mask to hide any sense of anguish beneath it (not a weird metaphor; I literally found a Beyoncé mask on a table). I accepted that maybe I wouldn't be walking again in the next few weeks and maybe I wouldn't be able to return to dancing the night away for a while. It isn't the greatest time to realise this when you're drunk. Intoxication puts you on the edge of your emotions, leading to one thing magically clicking you into a certain state of mind. It is a force so strong that it is almost impossible to click back out. I held it together. I hid the desperate disappointment beneath the thick layers of fake smiles I had become so accustomed to producing. I simply acted as if I was just a bit tired, as if my first night out in months had taken its toll on my energy level, not my ankles. I couldn't even tell Flo while she moaned at me for being lazy and annoying because I wanted to sit on the wall for a second before walking home. It would've been easy to open up then. To reveal every frustration and punch in the gut I had felt in the last month let alone that night. But I didn't. Again, I didn't wanna be that guy. I didn't want the continued jokes about my ankles to start because they represented something that actually personally affected me.

I just wanted to be walking. Away from the clubbing; the drinking; the singing football chants on double-decker buses. I just wanted to be pelted by rain as I tried to navigate a boggy field that encompassed my squelchy feet. I'd actually started to enjoy the walks. The new relaxed schedule, Sam's company, whatever it was... I felt like I was ready to finish this demented challenge I had set myself. It was no longer just because of a duty I felt I had; it was because I bloody loved the Norwich walk! And the second half of the Folkestone one for that matter. I had done 400 miles of walking since January, including my training, and I didn't want to fucking stop there. Six hundred more to go: bring it on! Fuck my fucking ankles and their shitting little pains! Why couldn't I just be allowed to enjoy this year and do what I set out to do? That's what hurt the most. Sitting on that wall. Five minutes away from my house. Pissed off my face. Realising that I probably wouldn't be able to walk for at least another month. Or maybe I wouldn't be able to walk again. I don't mean like actually *walk*, as in put one foot in front of the other. I was able to *walk*, just to clarify. I mean going on my long-distance wanders, with my wanker of a backpack on my shoulders. I know I moaned about how painful and endless they felt. And they did. I won't deny that. But I had finally got to this point of enjoying the walks: I knew what was right in terms of distance per day; I knew what was right in terms of headphones or no headphones (key stuff); I knew why and what I was doing the bloody thing for. Just when everything was coming together (all that insight, understanding and enjoyment), my ankles decided that it was time to subside into a state of permanent pain. Great. Amazing. You're the best. Love you guys. Fuck you and your shitty little joints and how they're supposed to work perfectly together without a problem in the world but in reality they're just a load of shite neither of which has a fucking clue what the other one does. Sorry. I wanted to walk and my ankles were shit, basically.

I guess that's an attempt to give you a glimpse of my mind, and at the time it was largely filled with feelings which didn't just wallow, but were drenched in self-pity, and a fair bit of repressed anger too. Of course, I hid this. People would occasionally see glimpses revealed as it's pretty hard to hide my frustration when it affects every step I take. My solution for the painful following day: get drunk. This was courtesy of my old charmingly beardy drama teacher. Not old as in old in age, old as in not my teacher any more (I'm not calling you old, sir. And I'm still calling you sir because I feel like using your name in this book goes slightly over the boundaries). With a few pints of cider and a few hours passed, I exited the pub with a slightly tipsy stride in my step. Just to please the man with the beard I shall give you this disclaimer: he bought me all my drinks and then proceeded to brand me a 'cheapskate' as a result of such shenanigans. I cannot argue. I very much didn't want to spend five pounds on a pint and it took me a few to start attempting to decline his offers ('Drinks on me next time, maybe just the one though.'). I then wandered off down the street at 7pm, drunkenly stumbling home with the aid of Flo, who had mysteriously appeared out of nowhere. The drunken stumbling class was real high at this point. After finding my house successfully, I wrote something. Sounds mysterious, but it isn't. That night I lay in my bed and wrote a part of this book for the future, something I kept far away in a hidden passage of my computer's memory so no one could find it until I attempted to publish. It's not too happy, again, so be prepared; it pretty much perfectly summarises how I felt at the time:

It's not easy. Having the only thing you had planned for your year, the only thing you looked forward to, fucked up. Yes, I know it's hardly a serious problem in comparison to the millions of others in pain all over the world. But I lie here again in my bed, tear stricken, wondering what the fuck to do. I have nothing to do with my life other than wallow in self-pity. Wallow in self-pity at the fact that I have already taken four weeks off walking and I can still feel the pain inflicted upon my ankles. Wallow in self-pity at the fact that I have let down every poor soul who sponsored me. I don't give a shit how much they tell me that I haven't. I have. I committed to something and I have failed. I guess that it's tough accepting that I've failed, failed at something that I barely started. Yes, I can still cycle, but it's not the same. It is a compromise I created in my head which would be the point at which I admitted I had failed. I feel the judgement of people who laughed at what I was doing, who called it 'ridiculous' or 'preposterous', I can see the smug self-righteousness in their eyes as they are proved right by my inevitable failure. And, of course, I will attempt to walk to Edinburgh but the likelihood of that right now looks increasingly low. The worst bit is seeing people, and the ultimate question: 'So how are the walks going?' I hit them back with the humorous 'Well, my ankles are fucked' to hide the shame and pain I feel whilst uttering such a line. I don't know. I really don't. I don't know what to say when my mum batters me with requests of what physio I want to go to and how I should call them up tomorrow when all I want to do is scream in her face: 'I DON'T GIVE A SHITTING FUCK.' But I don't, I just vacantly listen away before wandering off into the hollow shell of my bedroom.

I'm sorry for engaging you in my depressive mindset. I felt that it might help. In some way it would feel as if I was talking to someone about it. That I hadn't just locked it away, swallowed the key and shat it out in a distant desert. And, just as I am about to reveal the holy destination of the excreted key, I laugh; jump; run; tumble and scream until you forget that anything remained hidden. On another note, I feel depressed at this point in

time. I would search for another word to avoid confusing the two very dif-
ferent states of mind, but I do not feel like any other word can fully justify
what I feel right now. Yet I understand that the use of the word in lighter
terms can downplay depression as a serious mental disorder, because we all
feel 'depressed' at some point, don't we? No. We all feel sad at some point,
but that does not mean we are depressed. I cannot write eloquently, or prob-
ably that accurately, about what it is like to be depressed because I do not
believe that I have ever been truly depressed. Depression isn't just about 'feel-
ing sad' and something you can 'grow out of'. It is a serious mental illness
and should be treated as such. Whilst my sadness is, to me, a serious issue,
it is pale in comparison to those suffering at the hands of worse demons. I
understand that.

Do you like that I put it in italics? Classy, right? I don't really know
whether that's like the 'official' way you're supposed to do it but italics
always look good so fuck it. The story of what happened mainly starts
with my joyful visit to the white fluorescent halls of A&E. There
are certain ways to get things sorted more quickly in the NHS, and
going to A&E rather than having to wait months on a waiting list
is one of them. I felt guilty. Technically my injury wasn't an 'emer-
gency'. Maybe it was an 'accident' as I didn't just stand smacking my
feet on the ground until they felt weak enough to have a jolly visit
to hospital. Me and my mum were fed up, to be honest. I'd had a
lot of wishy-washy comments about what it was and what to do but
after the return of my limp, courtesy of the clubbing world and my
physio's not too helpful advice, I needed someone to just bloody tell
me what the fuck was wrong with me. My guilt over 'wasting NHS
time' disappeared at the sight of a deserted waiting hall. It was a Saturday, a day on which the NHS supposedly ceases to exist, according
to the government, so I expected more, not fewer people. Yet here
I sat, able to count the number waiting on the fingers of one hand.
Maybe the patients had just taken a day off because the doctors definitely hadn't – fuck off Jeremy Hunt you bullshit-spewing, career-
destroying barefaced-lying fucking twat of a health secretary. Maybe
I'm lowering the tone of debate by resorting to such insults, but if

you are harming and destroying thousands, millions even, of people's lives the least you deserve to have to deal with is a couple of 'hurtful words' (fuck people over plus act like a messiah saving their bacon equals fairly angry people: not exactly rocket science). Anyway, basically, the hospital was pretty darn empty.

A delightfully sprightly frizzy-haired woman did the kind duty of tinkering with my feet to find the faulty bolt. A human scan would not do the job efficiently enough, so the fancy intelligence of a computer was needed. I was getting an X-ray if you hadn't worked it out. Another example of the efficiency of A&E – it would either never have been approved or would have taken weeks to organize if I had gone through the doctors. The faulty bolt appeared to be the whole structure of my foot, according to Frizzy Fran. My bones are a bit weird. They move about a fair amount. Much like me, they seem to innocently wander around confusing everyone who watches them. Fearful, I asked whether this equalled some sort of serious problem: she claimed that maybe it would. She then explained in a full and finally helpful way that my injury at the minute was to do with the tissue in the tendons in my feet causing the inflammation that was clearly visible. Although intensely boring to repeat, this clearcut description finally allowed me to dissect the riddle that had left me confused for weeks. It was my tendons! I could now efficiently describe what was wrong with me to any passer by, and bore them to death in the process. After a quick decision to say a respectfully silent goodbye to my physio, we now had a cheekily arranged appointment with a sports injury specialist (fancy I know) courtesy of Frizzy Fran's efficiently speedy service. (She's not called Fran by the way, I just thought it sounded good.) Good treatment; nice chat; speedy service; better than a bloody physio we ashamedly had to pay for.

I do feel guilty for using the quite clearly unfair system for my own advantage. Of course, in comparison to many other countries across the world, our healthcare system is incredibly fair and progressive in its basic principle of being free at the point of use. However, this does not classify it as the perfect system – many cracks become visible as you delve into its inner workings. Like our education system, there exists something often named as 'choice'. You can choose to wait it out in the NHS for a likely waiting period of over five weeks or skip the commoners' queue through the loophole of private healthcare. However much people like to call this a 'choice', it isn't. It is a choice for those who have enough money, like my family, for it to *be* a choice. It is not a choice for the large majority of the population who cannot afford to pay for things such as private physios or paediatricians. For them, it is a waiting game on endless lists with no instant relief. Simply because they have less money, they are treated many weeks later even if their psychological or physical problems cannot be so patient. Pretty much sums up the fucked nature of our society in which more money equals faster and better treatment in all areas of life.

Another example can be seen in the education system – money means that you can buy your child a 'better' education. And before you give me the bullshit that is the argument that they award scholarships to the lucky chosen poor children to clear their conscience, think of who they actually award these scholarships to. Smart children. So if you're rich and a bit dimmer than the rest it's fine but if you're poor and not a child prodigy then you have to go to normal-people-average-quality school. This is not to diss the comprehensive system within the UK; it can be very much top standard, especially Stokey, which I was lucky enough to have attended, but it would be an even higher standard if the unfair and unjust system of private education was ended and such schools turned into state schools to improve everyone's education, not just that of the rich and privileged 6.5 per cent of children. State schools do provide a great education and I do not want to put them down in any way because of this. It is just that attendance at a private school both increases a child's chances of attending a 'top' university and their chances of being very wealthy in later life, fuelling the inevitable endless cycle of inequality that we currently have. So it is not a 'choice' to have public and private systems coexisting; it is rather a summary of how money and privilege can buy you a better life in the beautifully unequal society we live in.

You can certainly call me a hypocrite, as I did, reluctantly, at my parents' convincing, use the private healthcare system available to me because of the luck of my family's wealth. I am. I will not deny it.

I abused the privilege the system affords me. Even the sports injury specialist that I was to see advised me to seek a private physiotherapist because of the wait I would have to endure for an NHS one. It could be argued that, by seeking a private physio, I was allowing someone who cannot afford such a privilege to see an NHS physio sooner by not getting in their way. This then suggests that private healthcare does relieve some of the stress on the NHS. This is indeed the case; I do not think that closing the private healthcare system is a solution. But I do think the private education system should be closed down, as although you can draw parallels (as I did earlier), they are very different worlds. The principle of equal education no matter what a person's background is much more fundamental and achievable in shaping the nature of equality within society than equal healthcare is. I was mainly attacking the idea that private and public healthcare is a 'choice', because that is a slogan invented by people for whom it *is* a 'choice' with little consideration of those for whom it is not. My other aim was to simply highlight the unjust nature of our society where more money equals a better life. This is despite being able to see no solution in which the stress on the NHS isn't increased by the closing down of the private system, which would mean that you are harming the people you are trying to help. Maybe there could be a solution in which the resources available to the private healthcare system are made available to the public system, which might work in terms of doctors but not in terms of funding. It is a simple fact that the capitalist forces driving private healthcare would not be willing to invest in a profitless public healthcare system. This leaves a depressing image: maybe, although it is in principle unjust, it is the best that we can make of the depressing world we live in where money and profit drive so much of our everyday lives.

Done. Promise you. At least for this chapter. No more half-arsed, off-the-top-of-my-head political rants. I'll stick to the vague confusion that was my life for these bewildering few months. A certain spirit called Murin suddenly became more important in my life at this time. Murin is an odd specimen; he is very much the 'loveable cunt' that he describes himself as. He is an absolute twat, not conforming to the social norms involved in being polite to those around you or caring whether people are offended by such behaviour. If he wants to do something, he will do it. Yet despite all the slight twattishness that accompanies his personality, you can't help but like him. This is once you get to know him. From afar he gives off the impression of being a selfish, ruthless bastard, but after months of having him residing in your house, you find he does grow on you. Slowly our friendship has developed from hovering on the outskirts of constant friendly piss-taking to a brotherly bond involving chattering on my sofa as we battle away into the night on the almighty game that is *FIFA*. So, with Murin, I now had a constant attendee at my house. Whether it was eleven in the morning or twelve at night, he would most likely be there. He provided a necessary constant distraction during what was a pretty tough few months for me, both psychologically and physically. My endless boredom could be cured by bringing the loaf into my humble abode. Right now, he has travelled to his distant homeland of Turkey leaving my boredom to arise from where it was deeply buried in its temporary deathbed. So, Murin, you have helped to make this year slightly less shit for me, and I am grateful for that.

The specialist. Let's skip to that. It was only a few days later to be honest. Surprisingly speedy NHS there again. I'm not going to divulge the complications of my injury or give you the in-depth stretching routine that was to encompass my life for the coming months. Lift the heels; steal kids' meals; you know the deal. Of course, I did not fill my lengthy schedule of nothingness with stealing children's meals. I did fill it with eating many of my own meals though. Anyway, back to the specialist. Must be nice to be called that, like you're so good at something or know so much about it that you're a *specialist* in the area (this admiration mainly stems from the fact that I do not feel I will ever be a 'specialist' in any particular field). After a bit of prancing and dancing about the room mixed in with a bit of foot massaging, he concluded that I had basically fucked up the tendon on the side of my foot and then the tendon on the top of my foot had tried to compensate but fucked itself over in the process. My tendons were fucked. Basically the summary of the conversation. Again I was given the timetable of six to eight weeks, a figure I had grown tired and less believing of. At least he honestly said that I would still feel it for longer and the next few months would be far from perfect. Cycling, though, was very beneficial and would be encouraged. So, I would cycle to Penzance and probably Edinburgh after that. This would be the long goal: it was now the beginning of April and the cycle ride to Penzance wouldn't occur until June. My next couple of months would be dominated by stretches, exercise, sitting on my sofa... oh, and shutting down an open-cast coal mine (we'll get to that in a bit and no, I'm not Margaret Thatcher).

Alcohol apparently doesn't really help. Tendons don't like it when your body is filled with what is essentially poison. Strange that. Probably a good idea to stop. I decided it was. Well, the specialist decided it was and I followed the advice. I had my mates back from uni for my detox so all appeared good. It wasn't rosy; I still felt intense frustration most of the time, but I'll focus on the good for now. A new physio then told me there was no need to see such an individual any more and provided me with another beautiful set of stretches to do. Again, this slightly confused me: I had been told to get consistent physiotherapy by the specialist, yet the supposed master of the latter profession had just informed me that I no longer needed it. I needed a distraction from all of this misery and confusion. So I made plans: I would visit people at uni; I would go to a climate camp and just try to make the most of what had unfortunately turned into a bad situation; I would attempt to be happy. Might as well give it a go. Heard he was a good guy.

The alcohol break didn't last too long... It wasn't me, I promise. The new physio had shot down the alcohol ban as unnecessary. I didn't just up sticks and grab the nearest bottle. I trusted the specialist's opinion slightly more, simply because he was a specialist. However, it meant that the detox would be weeks rather than months long. So, after about three weeks of no alcohol, I decided to break the break (ey ohh). Alcohol would be consumed. I would drink but wouldn't dance. This was wrong. I would drink and attempt not to dance. The attempt wasn't too successful. Despite spending the larger portion of the night dancing from the comfort of a chair (if you can't stand and dance, might as well sit and dance), I still strayed away from such a comfort to embrace the feet I had inherited to have a little jiggle

along. You're probably thinking that I'm a knob and a twat but dancing makes me happy and we were tryna be happy weren't we? I was
a twat but shush. I was sensible for the large majority of the night:
my bum occupied every available chair, even the one that was flying
through the air. People lifted me into the air on my chair, just to clear
that one up.

Oh, I forgot to explain where I was. I was in a mate-from-the-
year-below's house, which gave off the grand appearance of a warehouse. His parents are artists... Don't think you need much more of
an explanation. Anyway the next day the other side of my ankle, the
bit that was less fucked, felt a bit rough. It didn't exactly feel directly
painful but more like it was a bit more effort to move it properly. No
searing pain. Just a sort of heaviness. Like when you can feel an injury
even though it isn't directly affecting you through pain, just providing a mild discomfort. It would disappear soon, I told myself. I hadn't
walked in a month; surely it was on its way out. I was off to Cambridge and then some random Welsh hills in the coming couple of
weeks so I couldn't exactly worry about it too much. I would just push
on.

First up we had the wonder that is Cambridge (slight sarcasm
although it does get the credit for being beautiful). Darcy and I
decided to pop on a train to surprise our little Oxbridge boy Jack in
his superior surroundings. His delight at seeing us was rather limited by the fact that he was suffocated by the intensity of the insti-
tution that surrounded him. To be completely fair to Jack, he does
seem to enjoy Cambridge, and it's my hatred of such institutions that
breeds these slightly negative comments. Nevertheless, the trip was
fun. Maybe a bit too much walking; still fun though. At this point,
a bit too much walking didn't mean going on long strolls into the
surrounding countryside. No. It consisted of gently pottering around
a city of relatively small proportions. Beautiful things my feet are.
So, the old boys (my feet) had a fair few struggles but these largely
emerged afterwards. At the time, I distracted myself with the wonderfully poncey surroundings of one of the most 'prestigious' universities in the world. I put it in speech marks because it depends what
you define prestigious as. If your definition focuses on an academic,

and not creative, outlook then the intense, psychologically debilitating workload that epitomises Cambridge and Oxford could quite easily put those universities into that bracket. However, if you believe that mental breakdowns and intense stress aren't your type of thing then maybe other places are better suited to the 'prestigious' definition. You can probably tell which category I fall into – I definitely don't have any bias at all. I'm doing what is basically drama (Writing, Directing and Performance) at York so I guess I would fit more into the creative side of things, although don't try to make me paint or draw anything because I'd probably create something more resembling a donkey's shite than any sort of masterpiece. I'll stick to the acting. I don't think I've mentioned that yet. That acting is basically like the best thing in my life. Should we have a paragraph on it? Yeah, let's go.

Drama was always like a secret passion of mine. As I fucked around with my friends during the futile first three years of secondary school, I secretly adored it. Not just the fucking around with friends, which was pretty fun, but the feeling it gave when you could let everything out under the pretence of being another person. It is no exaggeration to say GCSE Drama changed both my life at the time and for the future. Drama gave me something I seriously lacked: confidence. I was the quiet child throughout my school years, the boy who sat in the corner and got on with his life, occasionally communicating with his mates. No one would've described me as exactly 'out there'. This gradually changed over the course of GCSEs and can mostly be attributed to the beauty that is drama. I would open myself up into the realm of putting everything I felt inside onto the blank canvas of a character. This is why I preferred dramatic acting to comedic acting; for me it was not about difficulty or what I was better at. It was a sort of therapy; it kept me sane as I stumbled through the struggles and troubles of life.

There is a large part of me that believes the pain I was struggling with throughout the walking year was not new; it had dwelt inside me for a long time. Previously, acting had poured it out onto the stage in front of me. Making it unnecessary for me to reveal such emotions to anyone around me. Now, having not acted in over a year, I was being slowly suffocated by these emotions begging to be released from the body they had inhabited for too long. I needed to act. I'd believed that taking a year away from it would be OK. It wasn't. I wanted to scream every feeling or twitch I had onto a stage in front of me because then I wouldn't have to talk about such feelings. I would simply show people. They wouldn't judge me; they would believe it to be simply a character I was playing, not me.

I will not paint all actors with the same brush, but for me acting was not a hobby. It was not even a career. It was literally everything. It was something I loved but something that also solved the psychological problems I endure. This was why I ran about my house acting out arguments, monologues, sketches, with screaming, shouting, sobbing, sighing, laughing and even the occasional dying overheard by my neighbours. I pranced around my empty house as if a thousand cameras were pointed at the face that sits upon my body. Acting was my world – nothing was more important.

I could probably write a book about my love of acting at that time. I won't, don't worry. I'll finish in a second. If it wasn't for acting, I probably wouldn't have half of the friends that I have now. I wouldn't have Darcy. I wouldn't have Jack. Two people who have managed to both make me go insane and keep me sane over the last three years. I wouldn't have had the confidence to integrate so solidly into the friendship group that now encompasses me; I would probably still be the quiet boy pootling away in life with his small group of male friends to surround him. Now, despite many struggles and troubles, I am largely comfortable in the friendship group I have acquired. I am happy with the way things are. There you go, some positivity. You see, my life isn't all shite and more shite.

Let's get onto the thing that very much did turn my mood around following months of wallowing. After walking and wandering around Cambridge for a pretty hefty amount of time, Darcy and I sleepily trudged home with two nights of light drinking and late-night chats and a cheeky helping of theatre and film behind us. Such dramatic people we are. It was all very nice and cosy with fancy-arse teacakes to top it off. But Cambridge wasn't the catalyst for my change in mood. Sorry Jack. Wales was.

Chilling in the Mines

Merthyr Tydfil – May 2016

I've mentioned that I'm fairly passionate about the environment, haven't I? Winkity wink along. So, this then culminated in my attendance of a Reclaim the Power Camp taking place on the edge of the Welsh Valleys, just outside Merthyr Tydfil. My compadres for said trip consisted of Baby Raver Ellis, Bavarian Bear Sam and Dynamic Dancer Rivka. Our plan: shut down an open-cast coal mine for the day having had four days of fun beforehand. Before you say, 'Why are you picking on the miners again?' – yes, a bunch of reasonably well-off Londoners going down to a poor Welsh valley and telling them that their jobs aren't healthy for our planet looks pretty bad. But we weren't arguing merely for the sudden end of their jobs with no replacements as Thatcher did. We were arguing for a just transition to renewable energy, which could provide many more jobs than the 200 or so that the mine provided, while also not carving what was essentially a disgustingly huge hole in a rather beautiful hill: if you've been to the Welsh Valleys then you know what I'm talking about. And it was also actually a local campaigning group of villagers who had called us in to camp on their land. We were not against the miners; we were against their employers, whose only concern is profit and very much not the workers' job security. A transition at this point would in actual fact provide much more job security than the sudden shut-down of the mine, which was due to take place by 2025, when coal is supposedly meant to be completely cut out in the UK. So, I get the concerns and had many of them myself, but after looking at how it was approached, and with the encouragement to respect the miners as simply people doing their jobs, I decided it was even more important to protect the lives that would be ended or shortened by such a mine's pollution, including many from the local area. Average life expectancy in the local village was twenty years below that of other villages in the Valleys. Twenty years. Meanwhile, the new mine that was proposed had been hit by over 10,000 local complaints already, showing that this wasn't us versus a community but the large majority of the community versus the big corporation trying to destroy both their land and their quality of life.

That's always one of the biggest concerns of protest. It's often the people who earn the least and do the least damage who are on the front line. They are therefore often the ones who have to face and deal with the protests while the CEOs, hidden away in their ivory towers, never have to deal with such people. I guess you have to risk the chance of having a small negative impact in order to create a larger positive impact. By shutting down the mine we would create huge publicity and therefore put large amounts of pressure on the company to ditch their plans for a new mine on the land we were camping on, while also saving the planet from a day's worth of coal and the deadly pollution that comes with it – this part was largely symbolic. For me, the miners were the only concerning part of this protest because I understood why they might be angry, but every other part of the protest represented the kind of action that I wanted to finally take part in. For many years, I've pootled along the edges of the environmental movement. Going to all the relevant marches but never being able to find a way into the actual direct-action activism that makes the real major impact. Marches look great but are most often ignored by both mainstream media and politicians. However, direct action does the opposite in creating huge amounts of attention in the mainstream media leading to more pressure being put on both the politician and business responsible. Many environmentally destructive businesses may not care about such little things as ethics but one thing they do care about is their public image. That is why companies like Shell or BP, disgracefully, sponsor so many museums, galleries and exhibitions. This gives them an acceptable public face to hide the destruction they have left in their wake. So the only way to create change is by damaging that public brand, as Greenpeace have done so effectively through relentless direct-action protests over the last couple of years to at least delay Shell from drilling for oil in the Arctic.

Therefore direct action is the true way to have an impact. I wanted to have such an impact. I wanted to finally fully engross myself in the environmental movement and this would be it. As Sam, Rivka, Ellis and I set off on our coach, an excitement set in with no knowing what to expect. It would be an interesting few days, to say the least.

Darting past hill after hill as the coach wended its way down the thin winding country roads, every turning seemed beautiful enough for us to just stop and set up camp. The mine: it appeared. A chorus of boos suddenly erupted from the group of strangers around us. A dark yet strangely beautiful crevice lay ahead. It's the sort of beautiful where you admire the true scale of man-made destruction that sits in front of you; the engineering ingenuity that has gone into this purposeful demolition creates a sense of awe and disbelief. Destructive beauty. I have awarded it with this empty and meaningless name. Stationary diggers appeared like distant dots in the midst of huge cliffs of the not-too-appealing mix of mud and coal. Then, they disappeared from view. We turned away. Our only sight of the mine for the next three days would be represented by the gigantic slagheaps that sat beside it, another sign of man-made destruction disguising itself as a natural phenomenon. We were here.

We did not arrive at the camp; we arrived as the camp. A small number of people were already there, with a few of the main tents set up, but it would be mass action which would create the mini-village that would last us for the coming days. Collectivity would be realised in the everyday workings of the camp. Everyone would have to volunteer for a job to do, whether cleaning the toilets or setting up the main marquee tent – we would all be involved. After hours of putting down access boards and collecting wood in a nearby deforested area, the camp looked pretty good. I'll attempt to give you an accurate picture of our residence. First, there was the gate tent which held a woodburning stove inside its humble space – Sam and I very much appreciated this while on our gate shift until 3am, when frost would happily greet us as we arrived back to our own tents. Then you would walk past the self-explanatory welcome tent and the again self-explanatory kitchen tent opposite the 200 or so individual tents in which everyone slept. We then come along to the main circle of, guess what, tents. Media; legal; medics; wellbeing; action; whatever we needed, it was there. Finally, we had the main marquee tent which was used for various activities, from dancing drunkenly into the night to organising the all-important action on the Tuesday. We had arrived on the Saturday. This little eco-town now existed within the Welsh Valleys. The surrounding views of delicately flowing hills decorated by the occasional dollop of houses were truly stunning to wake up to. If you hadn't noticed, I was quite enjoying myself.

I will not deny that climate activists are a bit odd. I can probably be included in this description: there's something slightly surreal about them. Whether it's the random outbursts of dancing to drum and bass in the middle of the day or the decision-making process being based on jazz hands, it was all a bit different. At first, we would sit gazing from the outside upon others as if they were part of some other species, but gradually we would become converted to their alternative methods of living. It became normal by the third day to wave your hands in a jazzy fashion if you agreed with someone or something. The weirdness wore off and we began to embrace everything. The food, all vegan of course, was delicious and far from your stereotypical idea of what such food is like. There was not a boring moment. Every second of the day you would have something to do, whether it be collecting wood in the local village to meeting the community in the same village's town hall. I managed to learn about the intimidation of the Colombian mining industry on one night and about the ins and outs of living a self-sufficient life whilst squatting on a disused private airfield on another. It was a pretty special few days. But the Sunday night would bring with it a fairly big shock to my system when my part in Tuesday's big action was revealed. It would be a part a tad bigger than I had thought.

Confidently, and stupidly, I seized upon the speed-dating form and filled it in like an overexcited, slightly overweight five-year-old child. Just to be clear, this wasn't speed dating for a relationship; the forms were to put you into an affinity group of similarly minded people who you would stick with throughout the day, making sure they were safe. The questions burned with romance. Willing to be arrested? Yes. Up for a secret squirrel mission? Yes. Ever done a direct action before (ooh cheeky)? Nope. I didn't exactly realise in those fifteen seconds what my answers would mean. Rivka then helpfully informed me of the fact that they'd filled the forms in earlier and not given quite the same answers. They weren't so comfortable with getting arrested or doing secret squirrel missions. We held onto the slight hope that maybe these forms weren't so important in selecting the groups. We were wrong. They were fairly important. Well, they were basically the only thing that was used to put us into groups. You can probably guess that Ellis, Rivka and I didn't exactly end up in the same group (Sam was going home a day early so couldn't take part in the action). It may be a slight understatement to say that we were in kind of different groups. They could openly chat, with no barriers, about how they would be in the final group to wander into the mine after others had entered previously. I, on the other hand, had a mission so secretive that phones could not be in our possession when we were chatting about it. In fact, I would not be allowed to talk to anyone about it, even my parents. It may sound paranoid, and it probably is, but climate activists have had a lot of clashes with the police over issues such as the hacking of phones. It wasn't only the *News of the World*. This to the point where many activists in Paris, for the climate conference, had their phones hacked into and disabled. It is not something that is in the past; it is something that is very current.

One thing that many are still concerned about, but which is probably no longer practised, is the use of undercover cops. Many activists personally know people who have been abused by such disgusting tactics, where they fall in love with someone who claims to be someone they are not. They're just fucking activists for goodness' sake. *Undercover*, the recent drama, documents this although does so quite tragically badly. It elicited strong sympathy for the undercover cop while also building an awful unrealistic plotline throughout the whole thing. Anyway, all of this, and much more, had made activists incredibly paranoid people. This meant that, because what my group was doing was so important to the action, they could not risk anyone finding out, especially the police. Leaving me phoneless and very much in limbo for the coming days.

'I'm really worried about what I'm doing on Tuesday, but I can't tell you what I'm doing' is probably not the most comforting text to receive. Oh well, I was shitting myself. I will explain what I was doing by the way; it just takes me a while to get there. I would be in one of the two pixie groups: this was the phrasing used to describe the groups which had secret undercover missions within the whole operation. Our aim was to enter the mine at dawn, between 5am and 6am, to shut it down before the others came in at around 8am to make it relatively easy for everyone else to walk straight into the mine. The original idea that was proposed would be to lock ourselves to the equipment, this being ten- to fifteen-metre-tall diggers. We would sneak into the mine on a super-secret mission and dizzle-dazzle our way to the centre, somehow avoiding the security trucks specifically looking for us, before locking our arms onto the diggers – and pulling a fine old pose at the same time, of course. With my nerves higher than at any other point, as the unambiguity of our 'almost definite arrest' settled into my mind, I decided that drink was necessary to help me forget the stress. Some Eastern European DJ and punk rock band would help make such worries disappear with my mind flowing from worrying about how being arrested might affect my feet to how it might affect my ability to travel home the following day. Dancing was not exactly in my capabilities at this point, not because of my drunken state but because of the pain caused by the lowest part of my body. So instead I wandered dopily around before collapsing onto the side of the hay-covered dance floor in a drunkenness-accepting state. All was good. For now.

I would wake to the beautiful uncertainty of remembering what I had got myself into. With the acknowledgement of this reality I trudged to meet my group at 9am; it was Monday at this point, by the way, so we had a day of preparation ahead of us. The rest of my group would go on a recce as I, not wanting to overdo my ankles in the knowledge of the eventful nature of the next day, stayed back and decided to pop into the legal tent both to learn my rights and to hopefully reassure my fairly perturbed mind. I was informed of the fact that I would probably be arrested and maybe charged, but it wouldn't be so bad: the most I could get would be a fine, so no criminal record would find its way onto what future employers would see. I had come into the weekend with a willingness to get arrested, but my imagination had created an image of being one of hundreds, not one of fewer than a dozen. These warnings though did manage to bring a sense of reassurance to my mind. After an hour of jokes, advice and generally friendly conversation about the not so friendly topic of being arrested, I emerged out of the legal tent with a slight increase in confidence about the following day. I had now come to the satisfactory conclusion that I would be arrested but I could survive that with the knowledge that it wouldn't affect anything involving my future.

As I settled into this new state of mind, something changed. We found out that the workers would be going into the mine on a bus at 7am along a central track through it. So if we blocked that track then we would be able to stop the workers getting to the machines, therefore stopping all mining activity before it had started. With this new goal we would now have those arm connector thingummybobs you see on the TV where you attach yourself to the person next to you through a great big tube, which is bloody heavy by the way, creating a human blockade. The plan would be that the six of us would create such a blockade and be joined by a fellow pixie group of six to block the parallel road, leaving no access to the centre of the mine. I saw the effectiveness of the change of plan. Others didn't exactly respond the same way. An unnamed fellow member moaned about the 'authoritarian' nature of such a move because they had changed our plan without contacting us. This is what I see as the bad result of having the kind of anarchists who do not believe in any sort of hierarchy as part of your movement. Nothing gets done. If you reject what I saw as essentially a more effective technique simply because someone has told you to do it then you are left with an unorganised and ineffective mode of activism that hinders the intended goals. If this supposed 'hierarchy' had a good plan then just bloody do the thing and stop being outraged by every fucking piece of information you receive.

Anyway, I don't want to have a little rage against my fellow pixies: we all had a common aim and were here because of shared positive morals. As long as you've got positive morals you're kind of a good person. I emphasise the 'kind of'. I exclude the Socialist Workers Party

hierarchy who told rape victims to keep quiet to protect the movement. I think the Socialist Workers Party is a disgusting, misogynis-
tic and all-round-backward section of the left dominated, as many
protest movements often are, by old white men. So, next time they
attempt to lay claim to a march with their papers or apparently easy-
to-agree-with placards, politely decline their offers and tell them to
either leave their party or scurry back to their rape-apologist friends.
This kind of leads me on to one of my other concerns when it comes
to the activist world: many protest movements within the UK, especially environmental ones, are, sadly, seriously lacking in diversity.
Just go on one of the big climate marches and you'll see it, or attend a
camp like the one I was at where the number of people who weren't
white could be counted on the fingers of one hand; actually I'm not
even sure they'd number half the fingers on a hand, let alone all of
them. A defensiveness often comes over people when their movement
is challenged on such an issue, something I myself have sometimes
exhibited. This idea that 'it's not our fault that not enough people
from different backgrounds get involved' is often spouted. That's not
good enough. There needs to be an active effort to combat it and
increase diversity, to challenge the fact that so many groups are led or
dominated by old white men. You'd argue for it in all other walks of
life, in fact you'd fight passionately for it, so why not fight passionately for it in your own movement? Openly try and challenge it, don't
just say, 'Oh well, it's not my fault'; saying that makes it your fault. It
shows a lack of desire to combat the hypocrisy of fighting for diversity
and equality in all walks of life as a group of white middle-class people
– whose own power structures are in turn dominated by white men.
I don't have some wonderful solution to diversify the environmental
movement – or any movement for that matter – but surely anything
other than the current lazy acceptance of the problem will move us in
the right direction.

But yeah, back at the camp, the plan was changed. We, after a
slightly frustrating discussion, accepted the new plan and set about
deciding how we were going to enact it. After a couple of hours sort-
ing out our efficiency with the logs-for-arms we were seemingly des-
tined to spend the next day in, we settled on our plan of action and

went our separate ways. That evening we would have a cheeky meeting to go over the last few bits and bobs before parting, to meet again at the lovingly chosen time of 4am the next day. I could now return to Ellis and Rivka. Ellis couldn't resist asking the occasional inquisitive question to which I basically replied, 'No comment,' as even they, as fellow activists, were not allowed to know our plan. With a little bit of din-dins, which now involved queueing for about twenty minutes because of the ever-increasing size of the camp, I would be very much satisfied for the evening. I then found out that the kind of 'main guy' in our group, in terms of experience and organising, could no longer do it. Not exactly the most calming information to receive. I think it's best for me to keep quiet about his reasons. So, with a bit of a resulting panic – there were less than ten hours to go – we all ran around like headless hens trying to find one another to make sure we were all still up for going ahead. At first, it seemed like it all might collapse and another group would have to take over (which, I'm not going to lie, did selfishly relieve me of many of my nerves). But we all grouped together and with a new addition to our team agreed the wake-up time for a coffee, bit of breakfast and of course our grand old mission for the day.

Four am. I spluttered myself awake. It was a tad chilly. I imagined the extra few hours I could have slept for as I stared silently into the corner of my tent. A scene which would look weird with another human present but feels very normal when alone. Breaking the barrier of temptation to lie motionless in my sleeping bag until what you would normally call morning, I got up. It was still pretty much night. A dark haze sat above our delicately placed tents, but morning began to splurge across the distant sky to create a path of light for me to guide myself to the kitchen tent. A random man, whom I had not met yet, was pootling about amongst the pots and pans as I entered the very dark kitchen. Our head-torches suddenly collided in their beams of bright light as we attempted to work out one another's identity through these tunnels of confusion. We exchanged pleasantries and went our separate ways, searching for some sort of breakfast amongst the almost pitch-black puzzle that was the kitchen. Slowly, but surely, the rest of our pixie squad stumbled down the hill to greet me. We stood drinking coffee and attempting to warm ourselves up in the freezing surroundings with the delightful prospect of lying on the ground for the next good few hours. When I say freezing, I don't mean freezing as in 'it was May and it was a tad chilly for the time of year'. I mean it was bloody 0°C, with frost on the ground, and it was fucking May! If these people have to live with both these temperatures and a bloody gigantic coal mine in the corner of their eyesight I feel very deeply for them.

After a short briefing from a helpful scout – he was dressed in black, had a beard and was small, literally exactly what you'd think a sneaky little spy fucker would look like (not to call him a fucker; I'm sure he's a lovely guy) – we set off to the slagheaps that lay about 100 metres away from our campsite. We ran alongside the fence that drew the line between mine and common land, though my attempts were more of a hobble to try to reduce the damage I would cause my ankles. My fellow pixies would kindly ask about said ankles' wellbeing and I appreciated this, knowing that they couldn't do much else for me; our mission did involve running.

Over the fence we went – it was probably less than a metre high. We're not exactly talking top-level security here. Run! Run! An unspoken order had suddenly entered our minds as we clambered along the bottom of the seemingly natural slagheap. A helicopter swiftly swerved above us. Without knowledge of who was looking at us, we carried on, knowing that there was no time to wonder about the ownership of the helicopter or who was watching us. We caught up with the other pixie group, who had stopped at the sight of guard vehicles parked on the only path ahead. There were two ways in. The other pixies decided they would form a distraction and set off on the longer route so that we could quickly sprint in and somehow avoid the security, who were sitting in trucks. We had been warned that the police were highly unlikely to be violent, but that the private security guys had form for losing their tempers and not being so kind. So you can probably imagine that I wasn't feeling hugely confident about the prospect of running right into their arms.

We clambered and clobbered along the uneven surfaces avoiding ditches and streams of black water. Ooh, coal is a lovely thing! Eventually we managed to reach the path and sprinted straight onto it, past the security staff who had, conveniently, parked their couple of trucks on the same path, leaving them within reaching distance as they shouted, 'This is private land,' while we scuttled past, followed by a more reasonable, 'There's no way down there, it's dangerous.' I held onto the belief that this was a genuine concern; however, the rest of my group did not. They continued the attempt to descend what was essentially a slope of coal. The sight of a fairly sharp drop suggested to us that maybe this wasn't possible, so we turned back up the slope and ran around the other way. If I'm completely honest, I had no real clue where we were going most of this time and was just aimlessly following the others hoping that they had more of an idea than I did.

We then began to clamber down the side of another slope of coal (we later saw that this one actually looked pretty unclimbable from a distance, but as we were managing to slither down we didn't know that). I could see what I assumed was the main road and heard the others shout the same. We were no longer covert creatures – we had become sprightly sprinters. I would classify my movement as more of a jog but the others can definitely lay claim to the sprinting title. Anyway, we ran up onto the road with security trucks coming from both directions. I'm not meaning to sound dramatic here as it didn't really feel so at the time. I'm just genuinely describing what was happening. Maybe it was a tad dramatic.

After a second of hesitation, a truck began to half-heartedly push one of us off the road by slowly driving into the side of him. Always nice. This guy twirled away from the truck, and then security seemed to have a realisation that maybe this protest kind of had to happen because they clearly weren't bothered to go all out to stop us. Their own realisation that they were no longer attempting to block our way meant that they then just sat staring at us from their trucks. We saw the other pixies jogging along. Time to lie down. We found an area of road to block and set about doing so with our massive tubes. Up to now we had been carrying them, not the greatest thing to have on your shoulders while running. On went the sympathetically designed tubes. Down to the floor. Get all of the road covered with what were essentially not enough people. We were blocking pretty large vehicles so it was about covering as much as we could rather than the whole thing. I settled nicely into the coal- and mud-infused road. The sun was just peeking down on us from afar, so warmth was occasionally provided when the clouds helpfully decided to wander away from it.

I'm gonna be honest: it wasn't exactly the most extreme level of protesting, as our opposition had kind of disappeared at this point. They would occasionally rev their engines and start driving down the hill towards us before turning back again, faking their surprise that we hadn't squealed and run away. But ultimately they chatted kindly to our middle woman (doesn't have the same ring to it as middle man) and appeared very friendly. They even gave us a cigarette. (Not for me, don't worry Dad.) We would unlock ourselves and stand up each time the trucks disappeared over the top of the hill in front of us. Then the news came through that the mine had officially been shut! We undid our shackles for a little celebration before shackling back up with the glimpse of an occasional truck, and with the prospect of the other protestors coming in: of course we wanted to look like we had been slumming it for the past couple of hours. After a little bit of singing and a lot of me staring distantly into the delicately arranged clouds above, along the road came the hundreds of other protestors. All dressed in vibrant variations of red, they created a collage for all to see – from wavering dragons to gigantic inflatable silver balls bouncing above our heads. The red was to symbolise the 'red lines' of combating climate change, one of these being the extinction of coal, so we were literally going to draw this 'red line' through the coal mine. They stumbled over to us, stuffing food in our mouths, yelping at the sight of us and thanking us for what had actually not been too strenuous an activity. Anyway, we'd done it. Eleven of us had entered the mine and, however nonchalantly, shut down the biggest open-cast coal mine in the UK. I've only just realised how that does sound a bit impressive.

After a few more minutes of sunbathing with our heads pointing down the downward slope, we had this refreshing feeling of blood rushing to the head. Lovely. Gives you this new sense of life, blood swimming through your body, emptying itself into your brain. I'm pretty sure that's how it works. It was a delight. Well, after we drenched our brains, we decided to follow the red swarm entering the core of the mine where all the digging and shit goes on. The diggers and machinery had helpfully been left standing tall for us to have a little climb on. Every piece of machinery was either dotted with red or draped in huge banners and flags as we approached with the line of 'We love you pixies, we do' blasting out. I'm not going to lie; it was quite a nice feeling. Of course, I did the fake distracted face as if I wasn't hearing the chants because of the awkward nature of actually acknowledging a bunch of people singing at you. It's like when people sing 'Happy Birthday' to you. What the fuck are you supposed to do? Awkward smile, or look down at the cake hoping for a chance to blow out the candles to mark the end of this difficult period of social interaction. If someone can send me a solution to such a situation, I will be eternally grateful. Actually if someone can give me a book of solutions to every possible difficult social situation that would be much appreciated.

On with the day! We joined the others for a bit of digger sitting before descending into the deepest crevice of the mine to be greeted by, what a surprise, even more diggers and a delightfully polluted lake: it was black. A couple of hours of climbing, photo-taking, lunch-eating, drum-and-bass dancing and even football-playing throughout the mine went past. The security men even joined in the fun in the form of taking selfies and carefully placing our flag on one of their bonnets. And the workers themselves were far from these angry Welsh men that we'd been told about. They were friendly, smiley and incredibly welcoming given that we were probably putting many of them out of work for the day. Reports from the protestors at the gate told us that the miners were even jollily dancing around with them and had chatted very positively to *ITV News*. To hear this felt great. The concerns about driving this massive wedge into the community began to disappear and we seemed to have done exactly what we set out to do, even gaining the support of the miners with their little quip 'Next time we're on strike, we'll just call you guys' making my day. I don't know whether it was our message of being against their bosses and not them, or the message of promoting more green jobs for a 'just transition', or just that they were generally friendly and understanding people, but they seemed much more supportive of than opposed to our protest. Perfectly summed up by the waves that greeted us while we walked around their workplace.

The afternoon would be slightly less stress-free as the police had decided to come along for the first time in the day. Maybe we'd stayed a bit too long for their liking; maybe they thought we'd just popped in to close the mine down for a couple of hours, then take a little satisfied stroll back. Meetings were held. Many meetings. We separated into multiple groups to decide our next steps. Some would go back to camp, some would stay for a while longer. It was all a bit up in the air, with whisperings about activity starting up again in other parts of the mine leading to discussions about whether to go wandering around the mine or stick to our guns and stay still, knowing we were having an impact where we were. Enough with the constant boring series of jazz hands and clarifying questions. After many hours of standing in circles trying to make decisions, we decided to leave a few guys in the centre of the mine while we slowly wandered over to another section that had reportedly started up again to, hopefully, shut it back down.

Slight problem: the popo. They kind of appeared in front of us. There were a fair few of them. Not riot guys though, all normal policemen – well, we didn't know about the five coaches and many more vans at the gate. But these guys didn't seem too aggressive, although they did announce they would give us two minutes to move off the path. Of course, it then took us so long to make a decision in yet another 'meeting' that the police actually just decided 'Fuck it' and walked right around us with no communication apart from the typical recording device to enter us into their records. We watched as they entered the centre of the mine where the few vulnerable activists remained. Worry began to set in over their safety and wellbeing as they definitely didn't represent the most extreme of activists. Later on, though, we were reassured with the tale of how the police had marched towards them, but then stopped in their tracks at the sight of one of them performing her one-woman show about Colombian mining from atop a digger. I am not certain how true this is, but apparently they let her finish the performance to rousing applause from her fellow activists. I like to imagine the police joining in with the applause, but understand that this is slightly less likely to have happened. Anyway, no one got arrested and we all slowly trudged out of the mine to be welcomed by a cheering sea of red back at camp. All in all, a pretty great day.

Sleep. I needed sleep. Sleep, however, was not on the menu. Hours of speeches and dancing, though, were. I decided to participate in the speeches but not the dancing. Not the normal way round. My speech very much confused me. I just spoke and the drunken people in front of me seemed to cheer and laugh at every word. It was quite nice if I'm honest. Enough bigheadedness; all in all it was a pretty beautiful day, with tears genuinely filling my eyes as we welcomed UVAG – United Valleys Action Group – to the stage, pure Welsh joy flowing across their faces. It was a special moment; everyone rose to their feet screaming, 'We love you UVAG, we do,' and minutes passed before it was quiet enough for them to speak. It was their victory – they were the people who were directly affected by the disgusting actions of companies such as those involved in this mine; they deserved a good day after fighting so hard for so many years, largely on their own. As the night passed, along with my sobriety, I began to reflect on how my mood had changed so drastically. I had entered this campsite with more worries than I could count. I left with few of them in my mind. I was leaving relatively happy. It was nice. My ankles felt a bit rough after a very tough day of running, walking, jumping and carrying plenty of shit but this, for the first time, didn't really affect me. I felt good. That's all that mattered. Exhaustion and relief combined to create a rush of emotions in my intoxicated brain which could only be called positive. I needed this, I really did.

I Went for a Cycle

June 2016

Home. I had a few days to rest and sleep before thinking about anything else. You can probably tell my year wasn't exactly consisting of a lot at this point in time. Well, I did have one thing left to do. Cycle to Penzance. I wasn't committing 100 per cent to get to Penzance, but I would try, and if pain or exhaustion got in my way then I would succumb to their ultimate powers. This wasn't me trying to prove my ultra-fitness. This might have been an impressive charity story to tell but it was also something that I wanted to enjoy. It wasn't about pushing myself to the point of collapse. I hadn't exactly always enjoyed my walking so I wanted this to be different, to make it worthwhile not only in charitable terms but in terms of my wellbeing as well. This meant that I would give up if I wanted to, although my psychological desire to not fail also meant that giving up was not what I would choose to do. Sounds very selfish to focus on my own experience over charity but my fragile mindset was more important to me at the time. Appeasing my mind meant providing a cheeky little break for myself as my family's house in Somerset was handily plonked in the middle of the route. A bed and a day of rest was the plan. Along with the other luxury of one of my oldest mates, Matty, meeting me there for the final straight. Company is always good. Anyway, I was cycling because my feet were a tad fucked and I had been told that cycling would not do any damage because it puts much less weight on said feet. Sounded good to me. I could partly complete my original mission on a bike – this appeared an easier feat to achieve. There was just the slight problem that I only started training about three weeks before I was due to leave. It's probably a good piece of advice that if you are planning on going on a cycle ride consisting of possibly over 300 miles then maybe do a bit more training than I did. Especially when you are also planning on carrying a fuckload of shit on the back of your bike.

Oh well, I couldn't really do much apart from just start cycling at this point. I also kind of needed a new bike as my current one was pootling along with a visit to the bike shop about as often as it actually went out on the road. I once paid more in repairs for it than we actually paid to buy the thing, that being about thirty pounds, so not the gigantic amounts you're probably imagining, but still. With money running short, my parents agreed to pay for half of the cost of a bike and we would go brand new for the first time in the history of all my bikes. And my dad wanted some properly functioning bikes in the house for some peculiar reason. I hesitantly decided to go along with it as I would, reluctantly of course, receive a bike at the end of it. If you hadn't noticed, I'm being sarcastic. That bike wouldn't be coming along for a couple of weeks though; old Pootly McBootly would have to do for now. Building my stamina up slowly would again be the challenge, as it had been with the walking, with a tiny bit more work each day. Starting at the casual total of five miles before winding up to the slightly tougher twenty-five to thirty miles two days in a row. I was planning to do forty miles in a day on the actual cycle but I thought, well, I can just get into my stride while doing the actual cycling and it will all be absolutely f-i-i-i-n-e.

My feet. There were a few developments. After consistent hassling from my parents I got up off my arse and went to a recommended podiatrist. I was frustrated with the lack of apparent progress in the recovery of my feet as I was only days away from that wonderfully deceptive target of everything being all right and healed in eight weeks. The fact that I still struggled with walks longer than twenty-five or thirty minutes, with the all-too-familiar pain returning after about ten, worried me. I needed some decent bloody specialised help, someone who knew exactly what they were doing and didn't just cover all areas. I needed to know some actual facts about what was going on and how I could fix this.

I arrived at the podiatrist, and instantly they recognised both the uselessness of my current insoles, and the exact cause of my problems being that my feet sort of bent inwards as I walked. This meant that I needed to reverse the action through both new insoles and a regime of stretches. It would be two-thirds insoles and one-third stretches and I could be provided with both, albeit with a slight burden on my parents' pocket (this being the reason why I was hesitant, my health so often being weighed up against my principles throughout that year). Dr Palmer was someone who finally sounded like he knew what he was doing; actually they all sounded like that, but he was the only one who was 100 per cent right. He refused to give me a timescale as he said it caused too much expectation and wanted to see how it progressed, something that, as much I was frustrated by it, I understood and respected. I was then given permission for a bit of dancing and quite a lot of cycling in the coming month. This pleased me quite a lot. Again, I was hesitant. I had lost so much faith in doctors and 'specialists' over the last few months because of their different diagnoses, their completely unrealistic timescales and their often medically wrong advice. I've had quite a few health problems and doctors have so far managed to solve very few of them so, as much as I am a believer in science, I have experienced a severe loss of trust in medical professionals even though I respect and admire what they do. But maybe this one could change my mind...

Let's get back to cycling. It is supposedly what I should be talking about. All the canals would need to be explored. All the parks would need to be cycled through. Then I could go off. It wouldn't matter that I hadn't covered my bike in the assortment of goods, during training, that would adorn it on my fateful journey. I would just cycle off and it would all be good. It is a lie to say that I wasn't incredibly nervous before I started. I spent the night before thinking about the endless possibilities of my ankles getting worse, causing me months more agony, or of giving up and having to face people after yet another failure. I am not arguing that any of these thoughts had any logical basis, but I don't really think that any of our thoughts have a logical basis when emotions coexist with them. If you want to call me insane or at least the victim of severe overthinking, you can, but I think every single person reading this has had the same nerve-filled paranoid thoughts. I had pictured this cycle ride as a delightfully pain-free, hair-blowing-in-the-wind kind of experience. The picture slightly changed with the severe ache in my thighs after two days in a row of twenty-five miles during training. The premise of cycling over thirty miles almost every day made the trip no longer appear so delightful. Oh well, I would start with my dad, so at least I would have some company for the inaugural ride and not be left all on my lonesome.

First day. (I'm not gonna do an in-depth analysis of each one, by the way, so you don't need to be filled with dread in anticipation.) Willesden Junction would greet me as my start line, where I encountered a fellow cyclist who had just completed a night ride. We chatted away about our differing cycling situations before my dad met up with me and rode me away with the grand aim of reaching a campsite just past Slough. Slough. I'm not going to say anything. I really want to but I won't because I do not want to deeply offend anyone with connections to this grand town. Let's move on. Well, that was what I was doing on my bike. Moving on. Hey hooooo. Oh dear, well to be honest there wasn't a huge amount to say about the majority of the first day. I managed to cycle twenty-six or twenty-seven miles, which isn't that impressive. We had a nice time pootling along the canals as my panniers swerved from left to right clearly trying to find some sort of escape from the bike, or maybe it was my bike desperately trying to escape from the reasonably heavy fuckers resting on its arse. I basically had everything I needed, a helluva lot of stuff, on the back of my bike, meaning that it probably felt a lot like I did when I had the same weight resting on my back. Like a ton of shit that is. I understand bikes don't feel but have some heart guys, it was suffering. Luckily, at this point in time, I wasn't feeling such pain. I still had a fair few more days for that to come along.

After a good twenty miles of cycling my dad and I had failed to find the café he had been dreaming of so we aptly settled for the Sainsbury's offer, always a delight. A beautifully fruit- and vegetable-less meal of mac and cheese with chips on the side was then consumed by yours truly. For dinner, upon reaching the campsite alone, I went for the slightly more vegetably and microwavable vegetable lasagne (£2.35 at Sainsbury's, and not recommended) to recapture my soul with real food. (By the way, my dad had to go home for work – that's why I arrived at the campsite alone, not because he suddenly fell to his death or disappeared into the canal.) Back to food. I kind of created the following mindset: I could eat whatever the fuck I wanted because I was burning so many calories – it was almost essential, as it had been with my walks. Despite this, I should probably have still eaten meals which didn't only consist of carbs. Normally, I don't give a shit about what I eat because gaining, not losing, weight is often the goal. But I will still always eat reasonably healthily because of the food that I cook. However, this doesn't happen so much when I am outside of the house, that is, on this cycle. So I wouldn't be eating in the most fashionable ways. But one thing I would do was attempt to avoid using my gas cooker, so as to actually eat proper meals, not unsatisfying dry packets of Uncle Ben's. Microwaves would be the main way for this to function – well, when the campsite actually had a microwave. Of course, they're not exactly obvious campsite facilities; they represent the sort of thing people go camping to get away from. I didn't care. I'd cooked enough meals on that tiny unsteady gas stove to know it wasn't the most pleasurable experience. I also decided to buy my food along the way: when cycling, it's easy to take slight five-minute diversions for a nearby shop, in comparison to a fifteen-minute diversion to get to a shop when walking – that is, a thirty-minute round trip. Which, when your ankles are reaching unbearable levels of pain, is a bit of a challenge. Cycling wouldn't generally be as traumatic, I thought, as I plunged into my lasagne, sitting on a bench staring into distant hedges and listening to the jolly families run around the campsite. On paper, it was all good so far.

Waking up was neither as urgent nor as rushed as it had been on my walks. Then, I was in a hurry, not knowing whether I could make it to my destination before nightfall. Now, I had the whole day ahead of me with my cycling journey taking up a maximum of four hours. Leaving many more hours, in the longest days of the year, to fuck about, whether it be sleeping in, having a cheeky meal or just sitting staring at shit. Benefit of having a camera: you can stare at shite for prolonged periods of time and still look like some sort of professional as the SLR sits slung around your neck, evaporating the persona of a lost or drugged-up soul staring at clouds that would otherwise be ascribed to you. ('Look at that guy just staring up at the clouds.' 'Probably high as fuck.') Why is he still babbling on about cameras, I hear you ask? Because, of course, having a camera on you is the most important thing in life, more important than paying your rent or having a job? Bringing a camera out with you, wherever you go, is the utmost essential thing to do, so that if your eyes land upon beauty you can capture it instantly for eternity? No. No matter how much the feat of capturing a moment outside of human memory is impressive, I have slowly turned against the idea of capturing *every* moment. Many times I had brought my camera out to photograph a view before I had even appreciated it. My mind had not thought: 'This view is beautiful'; it had thought: 'This will make a beautiful picture.' Yes, I was doing a photography project, but I also wanted to be involved in my travelling experience and not simply remember it through a bunch of photos which so often distort reality into this fake picture-perfect world that can be far from the 'truth'. A photo captures one specific moment in time; it doesn't capture the feelings felt seconds before or seconds after. It doesn't capture the events of the day. It simply captures that one moment and it's your memory that provides the context for the image in front of you. Photos can create trigger-happy explorers who are, in truth, not explorers because they are so hidden behind this obsession with recording every moment rather than actually seeing it for themselves. Forgive me for the pretentious lines but hey, at least I didn't say 'rather than actually living in the moment'.

I got up a bit late. That was basically what I was saying. By late, I mean about 9am. If anyone's ever been camping they'll know that when the sun is on your tent you cannot get up any later than nineish because of the sauna that it creates inside your humble abode. However, this was late in comparison to the mornings of my walks, when I usually had to awaken before 7am. So, I had a slight lie-in, chewed on a nice little Mars bar and went off on my journey. I had thirty-six miles to go until the outskirts of Newbury. Lifting your extremely fucking heavy bike up a staircase within five minutes of setting off does slightly lose you that starting momentum. Oh well. Off I went down random country lanes and canals to pass calmly through Reading with a couple of nice stop-offs, at a tea shop on the canal and a delightful Caffè Nero in Reading. Nothing better than classic train station food when you're following a train line.

I was still kind of following the train line, just to let you know. I haven't mentioned this in relation to the cycle ride because the idea had slowly faded from my mind as that epiphany I'd once had on the train receded into the distant ends of my memory. Now it had kind of become something I just did for the sake of doing it – a necessity, just because it was what I had done for the other trips. Now I saw it more as an idea based on the desire to explore, and not an idea based on the desire to follow a train line (a tad less exciting). This isn't to say that I was being a great intrepid explorer as I rolled on down this seemingly never-ending canal. I would explore in the evening, in the period after I'd had a shower and before exhaustion took over every inch of my body. Throughout the day, however, I would engage in a machine-like routine of few breaks and lots of cycling. For those of you still, weirdly, waiting to know the train line I was following... I didn't really have a clue. It was Great Western. I knew that. The one to Penzance? I don't know if there's some sort of grand fancy-arse name for it. Feel free to send me the info if you're greatly concerned by the lack of it.

Enough train stuff. Let's get back to the day, as it didn't end as calmly as the previous one. So far, it was all going quite peacefully, largely because I was cycling along the flattest possible routes – beside canals. I soon came to realise that actual roads are a fair bit more hilly, and with a lack of food beginning to catch up with me so did my lack of training with these things called hills. The worst bit was that it was all on a main road, so my struggling and shaking at the side of such roads was occasionally beeped or sneered at – it didn't exactly inspire me to go faster; rather it inspired a response of 'Fuck you!' to the inconsiderate arseholes. Sorry, was feeling lost in the emotions of the moment for a second there. Anyway, the day ended a bit rougher than the start with a few episodes of shaking when I took occasional breaks at the tops of hills I had just conquered. They were very small hills at this point, so the future days didn't exactly bode well...

That night. Another campsite. Well, it would be an interesting mix of emotions. Again, I was relatively far away from any collection of shops, so after vowing to avoid the holy gas cooker, I decided that there was no other option but to cook an Uncle Ben's packet I had bought earlier in the day. I'd have to eat the goddamn thing. I then set about looking for this mysterious Sainsbury's superstore that the campsite guy had told me about. I hoped to god he didn't mean Newbury. I wasn't walking there. Distance – nothing against the place otherwise. I wandered down a footpath, hoping that I was correctly following his instructions, before realising upon reaching its end that it had not in fact been the right way. And then came my first, and only, breakdown of the cycle.

I think a mix of hunger for more food than a pathetic bag of Uncle Ben's and a general sense of exhaustion then hit me, and created what was essentially an emotional wreck walking through random country fields as the sun set on my whimpering back. My eyes became hazy for a few confusing seconds while tears began to roll down my cheek. I contemplated why I was doing this. Why I had started it up again when my walks had caused me extensive psychological stress and this cycling was clearly doing the same now. Physical challenges didn't appear to be the thing for me, yet I continued to punish myself with them – along comes the all-too-familiar twat again. It's often not your actual feelings that cause these breakdowns; it genuinely is a combination of extreme exhaustion and a lack of enough digested calories creating a concoction of feelings you don't understand. Many times I would have a completely fine day but be hit by this overwhelming collection of emotions in the evening. It was very much a mysterious journey.

'I don't mind being on my own.' This isn't necessarily true. In some cases, yes, I am completely comfortable with being by myself while I have things to occupy my mind. My cycling can provide a prime example of this; I am completely at home with myself when I am cycling away through the day because my mind is occupied by such an activity. However, when these things are done, when my activity (whether walking or cycling) is completed and I lie in my tent with nothing to do apart from read, a sense of loneliness does set in. A sense that I am a hundred or so miles away from any of my friends or family grips me, and knowing that I won't see a recognisable face for another five days or so. When walking, this was not so much the case. Partly because I was never away for much longer than a few days, but also because my days came to an end much earlier as exhaustion would do the honours and send me off to sleep. When cycling, it was the opposite. The summer night would creep alongside my tent at a much later hour while my arrival at my destination would have occurred many hours earlier. This meant that by the time all of my chores (setting up; washing; cooking; cleaning; writing) had been completed, which might take no more than an hour or two, it would still be much too early to bid goodnight to the day. The level of exhaustion would also not be that delightfully extreme point of collapse that the walking produced, meaning that sleep didn't come so early and easily. This left me to my thoughts for many hours. Never good. Never let me delve into my own thoughts without the assistance of a pen to turn them into some fucked-up dramatic problem that definitely doesn't resemble my own, winkity wonk.

Let's cycle on. At about 12pm the next day I arrived at a slightly cobbled path which my map had told me to go down. OS maps are always hard to read when it comes to the differences between footpaths and bridleways. Bridleways are paths which horses, and bikes if someone has bothered to make them cyclable, can go down. I feel like footpaths are pretty self-explanatory. It's a bit of a problem if you get stuck on a footpath on a bike, because you will often end up in a muddy mess of a path, with your wheels struggling a fair amount. In this case it wasn't so much mud, but stones. When I say stones, I don't mean little bits of gravel, I mean big blobs of rock sticking out of the ground for my bike's wheels to delightfully bounce off. I walked for the first bit, largely because it was uphill on ground which I would even struggle to cycle along downhill. Then came along a delightful bit of downhill so I stupidly decided to cycle down it. I'd like to point out that by this time I had lost my helmet – I left it at a garden centre miles back, so safety wasn't exactly covered if one of these stones threw me off my bike. It was fairly bumpy to start with, but then it suddenly descended into anarchy with big bits popping out of here, there, everywhere suspending me in the air for several seconds at a time. Panic had already settled into my face for any unlikely spectators to see. I then saw this one rock. My instant assessment of it was that it had the potential to leave me a piled-up, injured wreck so, with no ability to stop because of the pace gathered, I attempted to do a little slide onto the bike's side and put my feet down. This left me with a very bruised arse and the rest of my body inches away from going over the handlebars... I can't exactly remember how this all happened so the description may not be top class. At that point, I decided it was probably best to walk it down to the canal.

I can tell you quite confidently that that canal was definitely not meant to be cycled along, but as it was my only option, I carried along its occasionally appearing path. All in all it was a bumpy but relatively calm day compared to the previous one. The idea of cycling all the way to Penzance had been slowly slipping out of my mind with every day that passed, but one moment gave me that slight motivation to continue. I sat atop a hill as an endless train passed along the rail tracks in the valley to my right while a distant mist soothingly covered the valley resting to my left. With its gentle beauty, it was again a reminder of why I was so keen to escape the hustle-bustle of London and why even if I didn't make it to Penzance I shouldn't end a day early. Each day cycling through the expansive countryside brought ten times more pleasure than a day in London did.

I told you I wouldn't do a day-by-day analysis didn't I? Sorry, that may have been a lie. Well, we can skip a bit through the next day because that's largely what I did with the simple desire to get to my family's house in Somerset and collapse onto the bed that awaited me there. I didn't fully explain this bit. Basically the plan from here was to rest for a couple nights as my friend Matty would, eventually, join me in the cottage, and then for the following six days. I say 'eventually' because Matty's journey to Somerset would be a reasonably eventful one.

He had informed me that he was leaving at 3pm from Bournemouth, where he goes to uni, to arrive at the house by nightfall on the same day as my own arrival. Such a journey was going to be sixty miles. My longest day so far had been thirty-eight miles and that had been a fair struggle. He ended up leaving at 5pm. Slightly later than planned. Slightly more challenging. I did tell him that this was a high estimation of his own or anyone's abilities, but with determination (I'm not going to give you a ribbing, Matty), he fought past the doubters to end up in a random village about twenty or twenty-five miles away from our house at 9pm – this is actually very impressive progress. There was a slight problem, in that when he told me of his whereabouts, he was on the brink of ending it for the day. No train would arrive into Frome before 1am so, with this knowledge, his parents, like mine before, found a little country inn for him to check into for the night. With a more sensible head the next day, he jumped on the local train to eventually arrive at the house late in the afternoon, about eighteen hours later than originally expected. All this kerfuffle along with the fact my gears had decided to go funny – they were just having a bit of a struggle to change when requested – made me come to the conclusion that it was probably best to delay our departure by a day. Sleeping in a bed for another night made this option even more attractive. Of course it was mainly to wait for my dad's arrival on the Friday so that he could have a little look at my dodgy gears while also giving Matty a fair rest after his dramatic couple of days. Definitely not only the bed thing. So, we arrived on the Wednesday and Thursday respectively and would depart on the Saturday for our first forty-mile cycle across the Somerset Levels, which were helpfully very flat.

My dad would accompany us across this distance – he's quite the keen cyclist. Picture middle-aged, Lycra-clad man attempting to cycle up mountains when on holiday and you get the idea. In comparison, Matty's and my little escapade was minute. It didn't feel it, though to be fair to us my dad didn't carry any weight when he went on his cycle rides. Despite this, it was still very much not the same thing, but shush. The day would kick off with a joyous descent into Wells. Four miles. Constantly downhill. Fuck me. Probably one of the best few minutes of the whole trip. Hair up in the air; smiles beaming across our faces; soft warm winds bouncing across our bodies. It was the kind of downhill when you know that you don't have to worry about tapping your brakes because the descent is so long-lasting. Not a single pedal was turned as we glided into England's smallest city, only 10,536 inhabitants remarkably. Imagine a constant descent for tens of miles along a similarly straight road? Ahhh, it would be so nice! Sorry, I'm still lost in my love for that slide to heaven.

Is Wells heaven? Well, to my younger smaller self it felt like it; it was the home of 'that swimming pool with the rapids'. Any swimming pool with rapids is great, to be honest. It's just fun. Swirling around. So, yeah, basically that's why I loved Wells, not because of the beautiful cathedral or the cute little streets, but because it had a swimming pool with rapids. Although I do also love what I call 'the streams in the street' – those little sunken gaps between roads and pavements that water whizzes down on a rainy day. If you know, you know. If you don't know, you don't know.

Matty's love for Wells came from quite a different angle: *Hot Fuzz*. Wells was in fact the location in which the majority of *Hot Fuzz* was filmed. That barmy old town? That was Wells. I decided, at first, to keep this from Matty. Watching his confused face as he attempted to work out why he recognised the buildings around me very much amused me. '*Hot Fuzz*,' I muttered. His world was changed. 'The courtyard where they have the shoot-out!' 'The road that they walk along!' 'The archway they walk through!' This may not be exactly what he said, more like almost definitely not, but you know, it kind of gives you the gist. He was fairly excitable. Not a bad thing with thirty-odd miles to go.

After a couple of wrong turns added a refreshing number of extra miles, our arrival at the campsite was quite nicely timed with Wales and England's first games of the Euros. My dad, the crazy cyclist, decided to give cycling all the way back to the house a little go (don't ask why), only after buying us dinner and watching the Wales game of course. Slowly me and Matty descended into intoxication as we bought pint after pint to increase the entertainment and fill the agony of the traditionally disappointing England game, 1–1 with Russia, before stumbling into our tents to play a drunkenly confused game of Trivial Pursuit. It was quite an entertaining evening if I'm honest, and made me look forward to the rest of the trip. As I've already mentioned, campsites suddenly seem much more appealing when you aren't on your own. (And surrounded by middle-aged men who have weirdly decided that camping is an appropriate form of accommodation when on a business trip, waking in their tents at 8am as if it were a normal working day. I mean it's cheap and I'm all for saving that money, but emerging from a tent in a suit is not something I can ever imagine doing. They'd chat away to each other, engaging in the kind of mundane small talk that I really can't be bothered with. I don't mind listening to someone else suffer through it though, especially from the comfort of my sleeping bag.) Now I had Matty to shield me from any odd social interactions with people, although a lovely couple did offer us a cup of tea from their caravan after sympathising with our slightly less attractive tent accommodation. All in all, a decent day.

Devil Day. That is what I'd like to proclaim this Sunday as. Well, maybe the first half of it. We awoke with surprisingly little dust hanging in our heads from the night before. Packed up, we set off along the canal before stopping at Morrison's to treat ourselves with a fantastically cheap but also fantastically plastic breakfast – the mushrooms had the lovely tang of vomit to tickle our taste buds with. Onwards and very much upwards. This means hills. Hills aren't nice. I think I may have mentioned this before. But those other hills were horseshit compared to what we were about to try and climb. We calmly got up the first few. I say calmly; there were a certain number of swearwords emitted in the process. Then came the monster that would poison both our moods and the estimation of our own fitness. I had the knowledge that we were approaching a hill which would probably be unclimbable when you have the weight of a constipated donkey on the back of your bike. It gets slightly worrying when the front of your bike begins to lift upwards as you climb because of such weight. So, as you can imagine, we decided to walk it after about five minutes of attempted climbing. I hope you understand that when I say climbing I don't literally mean climbing up a cliff face with our bikes attached to us via a hanging piece of string. You probably do understand, but thought I'd clear that one up just in case. Climbing simply means cycling uphill, so a small climb is a small hill. I'm a proper cyclist I am. Anyway, we got off our bikes without realising that it would take the large part of an hour to walk to the top, whilst a Lycra-clad cyclist confidently breezed past us exclaiming, 'It's all about the weight,' with his coincidentally weightless bike. Tosser.

We did make it to the top, eventually. The ability to mount our bikes again created a sense of gratitude for cycling that I had not previously felt. We could glide along covering the same distance in five minutes as we had in thirty minutes of walking. Soon though, we came to realise that we were once again descending and the one thing you learn as you cycle is that when you begin to descend you will most likely have an ascent in the near future. So, as much as fly-ing down hills at high pace is incredibly satisfying with the cool air brushing against your face, it also comes with the knowledge at the back of your head that soon you will again be panting for life as you attempt to successfully climb the next devil's creation of a hill. So, as predicted during our descent, another delightfully steep hill came bundling along. This wasn't even the bad bit. The bad bit was the fact that I made us take the wrong turning as my tired mind for-got whether we had already passed a certain crossing. Unfortunately, such a wrong turning decided to also reveal itself as a descent. Even more unfortunate was the fact that Matty had sped off down it just as I realised that we had taken said wrong turning. Then, just to make things a whole lot jollier, it started raining. I don't mean a little tid-dle-taddle of rain; I mean a full-on shower in which you end up feel-ing like a sponge. Climbing hills in the soaking wet, what a delight. Nothing like it. Rain beating down on your back, eyesight disap-pearing as it blurs the glasses you need to see, and you, desperately attempting to reach the top of a never-ending hill. Oh, what a delight life is.

For a second, it stopped. Was that it? We looked confusedly at one another. We had just escaped rain on all of the previous days so surely couldn't continue with such luck. We were right to be doubtful. The rain started again. This time it was a tad harder. Full pelt as we pootled along leading to one moment where I sat atop a hill, hidden within the under-growth, hoping that it would all just end so I could go home and lie in a warm bubbly bath with no fucking hill in sight. Here's a little extract from my diary at the time to demonstrate such frustration:

Hills + rain = DISGUSTING X 100 – out of all combinations that this supposed creature above us called 'god' has created this is by far his worst, well malaria and HIV are probably a worse combination but you know what I mean. It makes you come within an inch of stopping but then either a downhill comes along or the rain stops for a minute so you can carry on only to be battered again seconds later.

Clearly I was loving life at the time.

Well it would be about six hours later... Damn. I'm setting you up like a hot honey-sweet chocolate box. Ignore that turn of phrase. Things sometimes come to my mind. They don't usually make sense. One thing that did make sense was our decision to stay at the Forest Glade Camping Park, despite its seemingly steep prices. Such prices would be forgotten upon arrival. One little question would change it all.

'What you doing cycling out here then?'

Our cheekily true statement 'We're doing a charity cycle from London to Plymouth' (forgot to mention the change of destination but we'll get to that later) was always met with kindness, and the man who stood in front of us went a step further. He would provide us with the delightful offer of a free stay and would even cook our dinner in his and his wife's oven at the same time as they cooked their dinner (the takeaway option was closed for the night). This is not where the kindness ends. Later that night, after tucking into a cheeky vegetable curry, we were playing a game of pool in the games room (it had a games room and an indoor swimming pool – this was luxury) when he approached and offered us a stay in a mobile home for the night for free because it was 'predicted to rain' and his wife had asked whether 'they wanna watch the football'. Literally how nice can you get? We gratefully accepted the incredibly kind offer with absolute joy upon our inner faces whilst trying to act graceful and grateful on our outer ones. I'm not going to lie, it was a pretty happy moment and I decided to grandly celebrate by paying the couple of quid necessary to access the internet. I know this was an incredibly sad decision to make.

I owe that campsite for my ability to finish that cycle ride. Firstly, because it reminded me why I was doing it and that people besides me did care. But, probably more importantly, it had turned a horrible day on its head leaving me with a cheeky little smile projected across my face as I lay in an actual bed. How things change. Just three days left. That was all. In three days we would be all done and dusted with 280 miles behind us (or behind me, more accurately).

With that knowledge at the back of our minds, we bombed downhill, away from the disgustingly bumpy Blackdown Hills. This bit was rather enjoyable, bobbing across the rolling landscape with little effort exerted. Field after field drifted past as we enjoyed the comfort of pedalling away with no major hill in sight. Occasional humps would appear but would be quickly conquered without a second's thought. Our paces as individuals definitely seemed to vary. One minute, Matty would be whizzing up a hill at twice my speed. The next, I'd be thirty metres in front of him, pootling along. This was kind of the theme throughout the trip. Neither of us appeared especially fitter or faster. We never really had to stop and wait for each other, very different to the family cycles of yesteryear... On such trips, you'd quite often end up with a maximum of one of the four other family members in your sight. The start and finish of the route would be the only times we'd all be together. My sisters would speed ahead, my mum would stroll comfortably along at the back of the bunch and my dad would keep me company in the middle. As I'm writing this, I feel like that seems a bit odd but I've never really thought twice about it till now. Just the way it worked.

The muchly appreciated flatness of Exeter and its corresponding canal continued our fine day. A perfectly placed pub enticed us with its view across the River Exe as it descended into the sea. It was 11am and after a morning of pure determination we only had three more miles left to do. With the picture of me sitting contemplating life as the water gently flowed past me, let's explain my slight change of plan. After the day's delay in Somerset we had jointly decided that it was no longer about reaching Penzance as, with one less day to do it, we would've seriously struggled to up the mileage per day whilst clambering over the serious beauty that is Dartmoor. To be honest, that was the main reason I no longer wanted to go to Penzance: Dartmoor. It was more infested with hills than any area we had travelled through before, but if we bypassed Dartmoor it would probably have taken at least another couple of days. So, wrongly or rightly, we decided that the new final destination would be Plymouth. This way we would still have done an impressive distance and I would still have a week to rest my beaten-down legs before my Glastonbury home-coming.

My quiet contemplation at the Turf Hotel just outside Exeter actually contradicted our plan: I thought about the fact that I *could* probably have reached Penzance with a clear schedule and a clear head. The fact that we'd just covered over twenty miles by 11am with minimal energy consumed was a clear example of this. It showed the potential if we had decided upon a longer but much flatter route; it was easy to glide along flat roads. The only encounter that had frightened me was one with two fairly nasty fellas called 'Hill' and 'Rain' (pretentious names, I know). So, without those two fellas, all would've been pretty sweet. Anyway, away from my conflicted mind, the plan was now to reach Plymouth, not Penzance, by the Wednesday (the current day was Monday if either you hadn't noticed or I hadn't mentioned it yet).

A final three-mile pootle brought a rather peaceful day to a close. The biggest excitement had been me and Matty screaming at one another about directions whilst attempting to navigate a pretty large road. Drama, though, would come bundling through in the evening with Matty becoming aware of monetary problems. He didn't believe that he had enough money to reach the end, so doubt set in about whether he could carry on. I tried my best to hide my disappointment at the possibility of him leaving by honestly weighing up the pros and cons of such a decision. We came to the conclusion that, with a lack of money and him not wanting to live off meal deals, he would turn back at Totnes the next day. There was also the added demand of need-ing to be at his brother's art show on the Wednesday that swayed the decision. Of course I was a tad sad at having to do the final day and a half on my own but I understood and didn't blame him. Although he became slightly less blameless when he informed me that he had left his lock and helmet on the train, probably costing more than the last two days. Oh well, I would just have to contest those last few hours with my own determination. I still had him for a few more hours of cycling anyway. We rode comfortably – actually that's bullshit; we did not ride comfortably. We decided to follow Matty's Google Maps rather than my reliable old OS maps. I can confidently say this was a wrong decision as we trundled across many roads which I would not declare fit for bikes.

Bumping and bumbling along, over hills and cobblestones, we slowly bundled across Devonshire countryside. For the first time of the trip my arse felt absolutely devastated by a throbbing pain. Cobblestones are not fun. Constantly vibrating as you go along, the arse is well and truly battered. Basically, Google Maps is a load of shite for cycling. It's got no clue what a good cycle route means or looks like. It just rides you along shitty little roads with shitty little ideas that it's fucking quicker. Well it ain't. By the time your bum's been given what I'd call a 'rough massage' you end up at least ten minutes behind with every inch of energy zapped out of you. If you're gonna put a cycle option on, at least test out the bloody paths you send us down. It's just logic. You wouldn't send a car down roads infested by muddy bogs or stones sticking out of them, so why would you do it to your two-wheeled friends?

Enough with the Google Maps hate. It did bring the benefit of guiding us into a rather dashing forested enclave. Dash me with trees and I'll fight away the fleas. I like cycling through wooded areas… in case you wanted a translation. The darkened centre, decorated by the trunks of majestic creatures and illuminated by dotted sunlight seeping past the blooming summery paws of nature's wooden sculptures. BOOM! Suddenly we burst out of the natural surroundings to land on the not-so-natural motorway. No thought could be processed as the speed of our wheels rushed us over the expansive bridge, past the single empty car that decorated it. We were in Newton Abbot. Just like that. The trees were gone. The detached houses had begun.

Spoons had also begun. Begun serving breakfast! Damn. Transitioning your arse like a smooth little buttercup there. Just to clarify, by 'Spoons' I mean Wetherspoons, not the eating utensil. In case you were imagining giant spoons dolloping Full English into mine and Matty's gobs. No, it would be reasonably sized forks that would be doing that job in Newton Abbot's Spoons. Breakfast at Spoons. I want it every day. It's dirt cheap, as always, and the veggie one even includes Quorn sausages. Fancy, I know. Not your bog-standard veg-

gie sausage, you know the ones where they're basically just mushed-
together vegetables. None of that mushing, just that straight packing.
(Odd stage of the book this is.) The breakfast was the perfect way to
spend the last break we'd have together. Full up and ready to shit it
all out, we made the shared decision to switch back to OS maps to
see Matty off in style. No more bumpy bottoms or muddy escapades.
Clean sailing across smooth surfaces. A statement which was relatively
true. It wasn't difficult, but it wasn't easy. It was all right. Rolling
along the A381 for those last ten miles, occasionally breathless, and
into my dad's favourite town in the UK, Totnes. Suddenly, Matty was
gone, and I was left sitting sipping away at my Coke in the station
café thinking about the comforting smoothness of train seats carrying
Matty back to his own bed. At least I did have a bed to look forward
to that night.

One thing that I did not want to do on my final night was camp
on my own again. Matty had shown me how much better camping
with a companion was. So, with little hesitation, my parents came
through one last time and booked me into a random person's spare
room via Airbnb. Before that though, I had to contest the weather.
Torrential rain. I perched on a hill, under a tree, looking down on my
final destination of South Brent as every inch of my bike and myself
became soaked through. It was one of those moments of contemplating whether to carry on and just resign yourself to total saturation,
or to get slowly drizzled on through the trees as you sit slightly protected from the rain pelting every spare leaf around you in the desperate hope that it will eventually stop. After a bit I decided it was
probably best to brave it and, with another short break in a tunnel, I
headed off to reach the grand little town of South Brent. After a further half-hour, in the pouring rain, of struggling and failing to find
the house I would be residing in for the night, I decided that the best
option was probably to go and sit it out in the local pub. So with a
J2O and pack of crisps I waited until Rachel and Lars, the owners of
the house, came home from work. With clear instructions in my no
longer rain-infested mind, I set out to find the house. Within a couple of minutes I did so and was greeted kindly by Lars. It all looked
perfect after those last couple of debilitating hours. Dried off, cleaned

up and feeling fresh, I headed out for some grub. The chippy was closed; the Co-op would have to do. Walking back, pizza in hand, with rays of sunlight splintering across the street in front of me, the hills of Dartmoor rising in the distance, it was a very different picture from the liquid-soaked one that had faced me a couple of hours ago. A bed, a shower and a Co-op pizza would be the sweetest end to a rather wet day.

Lars and Rachel were great hosts, letting me use their kitchen, and chatting away to me as I did, on subjects ranging from Glastonbury to their crazy friend who had been cycling around Europe for years. They then considerately looked up the weather for the coming day: rain. A lot of rain. From early in the morning to about 7pm. I couldn't exactly wait it out in South Brent until 7pm before setting off for Plymouth, where I was going to be jumping on the train to Frome; there would be no train waiting to greet me in Plymouth station as late as that. So I decided I would just brave it out as it was only eighteen miles and largely downhill, so even if it was horrible, it would only be for a couple of hours.

Horrible was probably an understatement. After fifteen minutes of cycling, I felt literally as if I was made of water. Every part of my body had collected its own little pool of liquid. Riding downhill felt like I was being assaulted by a constant barrage of BB pellets whilst my vision disappeared behind my rain-covered glasses. I decided to rest in a bus shelter, next to a very confused Polish couple, who sat staring at me while muttering away in their native language. They were almost definitely laughing at the baboon that stood in front of them. Soon, the baboon would leave them to again venture into the rain-drenched air.

Just to give you some idea of how much rain there was, I'll tell you about an interesting little event that happened to me. I was cycling down a main road, as casually as you can when it is pouring with rain, when suddenly what looked like a puddle arose in front of me. I assumed it would be fine. My pedals, as well as my feet, began to dip deep into water. Think about how high the water has to be to encompass both your shoes and pedals: pretty damn high for a puddle. Stopping pedalling was not an option. I assure you I would have done it if it was. In the water. Out of the water. In the water. Out of the water. It was a delightful process. I simply had to accept my feet's fate of being swilled in water for the rest of the day. Soggy rain-infested shoes are a real delight. British weather really is lovely sometimes.

Six miles: the signs were keeping me going a mile at a time with cheeky reminders of how long I had left. Those six miles did largely consist of not too pleasurable main roads but as I got closer to Plymouth the rain began to ease. Maybe I would ride into Plymouth victorious with the sun beaming down upon my bike. Arms aloft and all of that. Turns out the sun didn't exactly get the memo, but the rain did. Slowly the rain would disappear as I pootled into the centre of Plymouth. Through the university I went and out onto the final straight. I could see the station. There was no sense of joy or celebration in my heart, no pumping fist as I rode in. It was more a sombre relief as I slouched into the station seat and sat in my own refreshing pool of water. I had two or three hours until my train was set to arrive. Most people would probably think to explore the area. Maybe pop into a few shops, have a little look around. No. No such thing came into my mind. All I wanted was to sit inside, away from the bitter wet and windy air outside those sliding doors.

Fast forward a few hours and there I was, sitting in the comfort of a train seat watching as I passed almost every mile of my cycle route all the way to Frome. Although the seven miles I then had to complete to get to my family's house in Somerset was not part of the 'official cycle', it was one of the toughest parts with a constant longing to just be there and resting, out of my soggy clothes and shoes.

I had finished my cycle ride, but my next challenge would be Glastonbury. I had a week to rest for the grand challenge of gettng pissed in a pool of mud for five days. Oh, life.

Finished

You can probably guess from the title of this chapter that I didn't carry on and do more walks/cycles. If you can't... well, I didn't carry on. It's not because the cycle was this horrible disgusting thing that I never wanted to do again. It was largely because it didn't really make me happy and doing another journey alone, in not the most stable frame of mind, was probably not the best idea. I could stomach the constant asking, mainly from my parents, whether I was going to cycle to Edinburgh, and the occasional joke about how the family holiday in Edinburgh was now pointless because I was no longer meeting them there via foot or bike. Before you say it, no, I don't tell my parents/family about what goes on in my head. I don't really tell many people. But I've always felt more comfortable in revealing problems or feelings in my head to my closest friends. I guess different people function in different ways, and that's the way I do it. I'm not saying it's healthy. I don't know what is. Well, I do know *I'm* not, at this current minute, with my health going here, there and everywhere. Sorry. That line was triggered by the many doctors who have diagnosed me with all sorts of shit in the last year. Ignore it. So, basically I had decided to stop. Maybe I would do a little walk before I went to uni to finish where I started, but I would not be doing any major cycling or walking expeditions. Half of the reason was because I had already done a reasonable amount and could no longer imagine enjoying it, so the only motivation to carry on would be to impress others at the risk of my own state of mind. The other half was the delightful old tale of my ankles, which managed to re-emerge during Glastonbury and many more times throughout the summer, showing that I was definitely not ready to start walking long distances again. So I stopped.

I'm not going to lie. This year has probably been more stressful for me than the year of my A level exams. Back then, I would have the occasional breakdown through fear of failure in the upcoming stupidity that was my exams. Now, it was no longer occasional. It was more a feeling which set in and refused to budge, no matter how hard I tried to destroy it. Setting out day schedules; promising to not use my laptop until a certain point of the day; filling my room with Post-It notes of lines and scenes that I have created within my mind to seem as if I was occupying myself in some way while my ankles left me largely homebound. These were all ways to find an antidote to my head. Even this. I started writing this as a necessity to distract myself from my own brain, despite it turning into some in-depth analysis of the deepest chasms within such a brain. I have not revealed to you all the thoughts that I think or the feelings that I feel, just that they have not been the brightest of sparks within my head this year. I would like to keep it that way. This, of course, sounds ridiculous. How are you supposed to understand my mindset without me explaining what it is? Well you're just gonna have to I guess.

Although I feel that this book is the most open I have ever been, even if it has been confided to a laptop, it may still not appear so open because of my lack of willingness to jump over that final barrier protecting the glass wall I hide behind. I think the reason behind my own and many others' (mainly guys') unwillingness to reveal these things is because of the stigma that comes with it. Men have been trained to be these stable, emotionless creatures who cannot let thoughts which involve sadness or anger into the open. How the fuck is that supposed to help? Why do you think groups of men, who are wankers by the way, go out on nights out seeking fights and to 'fuck someone up'? It's not necessarily because they are just wankers; it probably arises out of the fact that they have built up many emotions they do not wish to speak of because of this social stigma. This leads to the overclogging of minds, the need for some sort of emotional release, and for many this is supposedly achieved by beating another human to a pulp. For me, I can do this by projecting it onto a stage. We all have our little ways of dealing with the fact that mental health problems are not seen as legitimate in our society and are left to build up inside our minds. It is perfectly reasonable for someone to say to their friends that they can't come out because of some sort of physical illness. Yet we hesitate when the illness is inside our head. Have you ever heard someone say to a group of people that they're not coming out because they're 'feeling sad'. We are ashamed to say such things because in our society it is a taboo.

In men, this is ingrained into minds from a young age. It is not manly to sit crying in the arms of your best mate; it is not manly to feel as if the world is collapsing in on you. No wonder suicide is the single biggest killer of men under forty-five. Stacking up every emotion on a faraway shelf within your own mind will at some point become overwhelming to the point where you are left in a swamp of your emotions, unable to escape. I do not believe that women are naturally more emotional. I believe that it has been determined by environmental factors: for women it is seen as this natural thing because society allows and expects women to express their emotions. While men are taught that emotions should be left to women, as if we do not feel those emotions. Slowly, there appears to be an acceptance within modern society that maybe this was a wrong perception. However, when I say slowly, I mean incredibly slowly. Even as I write this, seeming like I understand the problem, I am part of the problem. I pen in every emotion and even with the perfect opportunity, such as this, I am only willing to reveal snippets in the fear that people will judge me for what is going on within my head. That I will be seen as some sort of cry-baby or emotional wreck by everyone who decides to read this. Mental health problems are not some twenty-first-century creation by people who want to justify their own overwhelming 'emotions'; they are a serious issue within our society, and I believe almost every person, especially men, suffer from them at some time or other, even if in the most minuscule ways.

Wooowee... Sorry for that intense little exploration of my thoughts on mental health. Actually, maybe I shouldn't be apologising. I shouldn't have to justify my own feelings and apologise for them. I have done so throughout this book every time I reveal an emotion, out of fear that I will be seen as wallowing in my own feelings. But maybe we shouldn't apologise for such things. If you don't like it then fuck off and stop reading. Still, let's move on. Where should we go? Maybe reviewing the year as a whole is a good idea.

If I could start over, I would probably change a fair few things. Firstly, I would tell myself that my journeys weren't about impressing others with ambitions involving some significant distances just because I had committed to do the whole thing for charity. Originally, I had simply planned that I would just be wandering around the UK. Maybe I would do five miles one day, maybe fifteen the other. It would be an intrepid adventure where I would have no serious destination – I would simply follow the railways and see where this took me as I traipsed across the countryside with my little tent. If I had stuck to this idea, and not turned it into the ridiculous commitment of making many different journeys involving a definite destination and time period to get there in, then there's a chance that my ankles wouldn't have got fucked and my year wouldn't have gone to shit. These are of course just my thoughts, and there is no way of knowing what would've happened to my ankles, but walking over 400 miles in two and a half months probably didn't help too much.

Despite what I said earlier in the book, I would still do it for charity. I would just not let that overwhelm my plan; it would simply be an addition to what I was already doing. I had felt this pressure to impress people by saying I was walking to Edinburgh out of the desire to gain more sponsorship and therefore more funds for Renewable World. I shouldn't have cared. I should've just done what I wanted to do, and not given a shit about whether that would make people sponsor me, or whether they would be disappointed in me if I didn't do everything I said I would. Hindsight is a devilish thing. This is why, after so many months of being in that mindset, I decided to break it and not carry on, after Plymouth. Because for me that was the best thing to do. I just wish that I had realised it months ago when I was trooping about doing twenty miles a day on my way to Brighton. Unfortunately I didn't, and here I am with a still slightly painful ankle in September. Hey ho, the past is what it is, the past. I have learnt many things, like cooking by the side of a main road on a little gas cooker is probably not a good idea. Or that going it alone is not the greatest idea either. As much as I'd like to say that I could do it all on my own because I am that free-spirited person who will wild camp whenever he wants (doing that alone shit-scares me), who will go on this mystical adventure alone, and think of it all as the funnest thing I have ever done... it's just not me. All of it may just not be me. But I actually feel like this may be the case for a big majority of people.

FINISHED

You romanticise the idea that going off on your own exploring, travelling through stunning landscapes to the ends of the Earth, will be this great adventure. Whether it be wandering the globe on trains, planes and buses, or just pootling around the UK like me. You see it as this mystical experience. You don't think about the idea of loneliness setting in. The idea that, as beautiful as the scene in front of you is, it would be ten times more beautiful if you had someone to share it with. You don't think about the cold wet nights lying in your tent wishing you could just have someone to chatter away to, that your company wasn't just a book, a camera and a bottle of water (maybe this is kinda more about my walks than other people's adventures now). Don't get me wrong; travelling alone may work for you, but this romantic view of everything being perfect will at some point be shattered by the longing to see a familiar face. I'm not this great explorer who can talk to any stranger and instantly become best friends. I'm an awkward nineteen-year-old boy who plots out minute details of conversations in his head, who finds new humans to be confusing, mysterious creatures impossible to understand. Somehow this boy has managed to pick up some pretty great friends along the way. Therefore the dream-like idea that I could be this fantastical being sharing life with every stranger around every corner is false. I'm simply not that guy.

Originally, I didn't intend this book to be what it has turned out to be. I set out wanting to simply accompany my photos with a few chapters of me chatting away, attempting to make jokes, just to fill the pages. Now, it has become something a tad more intense. I have willingly put things on a page that I would only have done before if it was behind the mask of a character. I guess in many ways this is progress for me. It is mainly because those characters have not been present in the last year of my life: I have not done any serious acting or writing for theatrical purposes. And this is what has led me here. This book has filled the void that was opened up by a lack of acting; of course, many cracks have been left, and the void has not been filled to the brim. But it has done a good job.

An update on where I am as I finish is probably a good idea. My ankles have improved. This does not mean they are fine. Holidays or

137

long periods of walking or standing often bring the pain back into my life, lingering for a day or two. But I have managed to survive weeks filled with club nights, Glastonbury and even twenty minutes of not-so-serious football without the severe pain I had been in previously. For me, that is progress. It is still frustrating: I have many moments where I do wish that I could start this year again and forget about the walking and the cycling and just live without the constant worrying about whether my ankles will feel good enough to do something. These are short-lived periods of anger and exasperation, during which I think things that do not represent my actual thoughts at saner intervals. Honestly, I do not regret this year. At this current minute one ankle is feeling a bit sore again. I have just returned from a holiday in Amsterdam in which a large proportion of time was spent aimlessly walking around, always the best type of walking around. So that and the extra level of activity that I had been doing the week before may be a reason for the aching. Most of my time this year has been spent in my house, so the periods in which I have a few days of intensive on-my-feet stuff create a reaction in my ankles because they are so used to little or no walking in a day. Many people look at me mystified by the fact that my ankles are still hurting: 'It's been so long.' Sometimes I want to respond with my main thought of 'I know that very well thanks', but instead I try to explain why it has been so long. In doing so, I often mystify myself. I am not completely certain about the exact reasons my ankles have taken so long to recover but I believe it is a mix of occasional setbacks from overuse, the opening up of a recurring problem in my feet, and the general fact that their structure looks like it has been designed by a monkey on acid.

I haven't really talked of the positives in this little review of the year. There were positives. Don't get me wrong. It wasn't all just a prolonged sob story. Most moments of happiness were created by others, not myself. Whether it was my first night on the road, in which I was handed pancakes on a plate at the Redhill vicarage by its lovely inhabitants, or that night of beautiful music that me and Sam experienced in the distant village of Finningham. There were so many little moments that kept me going. Dancing across the North Downs to Justin Timberlake; contentedly staring across flooded Norfolk fields with a gentle coating of sunlight; screaming with relief and happiness at the sight of Brighton because I had actually fucking done it; or the drunken hysterics that set upon me and Matty as we attempted to play Trivial Pursuit in a tiny tent in Taunton. If it was just a big ball of shit, I wouldn't have been able to carry on for so long. I would've given up straight away because, despite my constant fear of disappointing others, I could not have survived walks dominated by misery. Little moments would help me fight on and push through the most miserable of times. The many nights residing in pubs or even the free mobile home on my cycle ride created a sense of adventure in me which led to a willingness to continue. Without Matty coming to save me for that second half of my cycle, I wouldn't have been able to do it. I had had enough of staying in campsites all on my own and Matty's company helped me continue. As time passes on, so do the worst memories. Gradually the gloom within the picture begins to fade to be slowly replaced by brighter images and fonder memories. I begin to miss it, miss the days of walking across random hills, looking out across the never-ending expanse of fields in front of me. Miss the days of gently pedalling along as the countryside whizzes past and my gaze is fixed upon the peculiar sights surrounding me.

It's odd. Memories seem to always slowly evolve from being negative to positive. Suddenly you can no longer quite remember that moment when you were crying in a campsite toilet while attempting to cook a packet of Uncle Ben's on a gas cooker. Instead, you remember the romantic experience of wandering across moors in the sunlight. I'm not sure if this is just me or a thing that happens to everyone. An example can be seen in my holiday with twenty of my mates in Sicily (stupid number, I know). At the time, I didn't have this unforgettable experience that everyone had built it up to be. It just all felt a bit 'meh' if you get what I mean. But, when I look back on it now, I remember fondly the moments around the pool doing all sorts of random shit and have forgotten that, soon after being back, I simply described it as 'decent'. Now, I see it as a lovely little holiday. I am confused by the reason for this, yet it appears to happen so often. My brain coats over these negatives leaving only the positives in sight.

That is why sometimes after a period of reflection I wish to jump straight back on the horse, forgetting the many moments of torment that I had put myself through. Whenever I am tempted to begin another adventure, I have this previously written paragraph to remind myself that it wasn't the smooth tranquil experience that I like to remember:

There were tough moments. There were moments where I couldn't stop bawling my eyes out. Because I'd gone past that level at which I could stay sane, pushed through that barrier that held everything back. I would scream; shout; cry; lie; and still it would carry on as if my unwavering emotions had no effect. It wasn't about drying out my body of every feeling it held. It would suck every little inch out and then search every nook and cranny for the leftovers. I didn't understand. Wishing away that I did, why my body would repeatedly punch me in the gut so that every little drop would spill out. Why would tears roll down my face when I saw no reason for me to be upset? Days when I had been happy, when my spirits had been up not down. Even those would many a time end locked in emotions I didn't understand. I wish I could unlock every reason behind every breakdown to block the chance of it ever repeating itself. I think everyone wishes that. That they could understand the pain they were feeling. So they could eradicate it as quickly as it arrived, so that they didn't have to feel like every wall around them was falling to the floor beside them. The cover you tried so hard to protect falls down without a single question. Confused, you retreat into a hole, not wanting anyone to see the fallen man that was once hidden so far away.

Oh dear, even my positive bit turned into a negative. Didn't I start with a bit of humour? I feel like this story kind of lost its comedic base a while ago. Anyway, let's ignore the confused witterings of my mind and let this tale come to its needed end. Let's hand it over, before it's too late, to my final little paragraph to give you the ending you deserve.

I won't deny it: many parts of me are willing to write off this year as one which resembles a pile of shit. For large parts of it I was unhappy, taken aback by desperate thoughts encroaching on my brain. I wished and begged for uni to arrive at my door. But, upon reflection, I would not bury this year in my unconscious (bringing in that cheeky bit of Psychology AS level there). Throughout the year, there were many moments where I did feel I was doing something special, something unique. A sense of happiness or enjoyment at such a fact. If I could do it all again I would. People doubt that. Because it wasn't exactly the most successful or pain-free experience. But knowing that now doesn't change anything. I still would've wanted to explore random bits of the country that I never would have imagined doing. I now know where the fuck Forncett St Peter is. I mean, who knows where the fuck that is, apart from its own hundred or so inhabitants? If you do know where it is, well done, but I think you might have a bit too much time on your hands. So, yes, it didn't turn out to be everything I expected it to be, but I won't forget what I did. As pretentious as it sounds, I will always remember the bullshit that I dealt with this year. I've said pretentious quite a lot to be honest. It's mainly an attempt to cover up the fact that I am your typical pretentious arsehole. If I say that I'm being pretentious then of course that will mean I understand the twat I sound like, won't it? When in actual essence I wish I could say those sorts of things without being ashamed of the wankiness behind them. But yeah, overall, a decent year. Hope you enjoyed exploring my mind – I probably won't be back.

Epilogue: A Couple of Years Later

Ooooh sorry. You're not quite done… I'M BACK!

It feels like a long time since I was dragging myself across the fields of Sussex. Almost two years if we're counting. I'm now in my second year of uni, a fair distance away from those cold February mornings wishing I didn't have to wiggle out of that cosy sleeping bag. That said, it is currently a cold December day and snow is falling on the other side of my window. But I'm in a house not a tent, and a cosy bed not a reasonably warm sleeping bag. A tad different. I've decided to give a little update on where I am now. What I'm doing; how I'm doing; how the old feet are struggling through life. Because as much as I can try to say that I have not written a book that is basically just about me and my life, I accidentally have. Writing this, outside the context of my year off, feels odd, slightly invasive and strange. Before, when I was talking about myself, it was under the guise of what I was doing in terms of the walks or cycles. Now, I have no guise or protection. I am literally just blurting out words about my life. Although I will be talking about my feet, and their original disintegration did occur on my walks. THERE IS A LINK! OK, we can start now. All is saved. Well not Johnny Depp's career but, oh well, who gives a shit?

My ankles. I feel like the problem is more to do with my feet but saying 'my feet' sounds a bit odd; you'll just start picturing a pair of feet and no one wants that. Well, maybe some people do… Foot fetishes aside, my feet (stop it) are sadly still not in perfect condition. It might not be sad for you but it kind of is for me. It's all a bit random. Some days, I seem absolutely fine, all ready to go and climb the nearest sub-standard hill. Then, out of the blue, a sharp pain will shoot through the buggers and cut short any hopes of sub-standard hill-climbing. It lingers, like the next step could bring with it another dose of heightened pain and limping. Not the best combination. On other days, I have this constant generic aching feeling lurking in my bones that I can't seem to shake. I can wiggle the old feet around as much as I want to try and rid them of it, but it stays, taking up permanent residence for the next several days at the very least. I don't know if this makes any sense to you. The truth is, until recently, it didn't really make any sense to me. The explanation: I have pronated feet. They are flat and over-pronate a lot. 'What on earth am I talking about?' I hear myself ask. Basically, my feet like to bend inwards a lot, which is normal but my boys like to do it a bit too much, hence the 'over-pronation'. This has left me susceptible to overuse injuries and walking 400 miles in under three months maybe, probably, counts as 'overuse'. Hopefully that sort of clears it up for you... It doesn't fully explain why I'm still struggling to get my feet anywhere near to where they were before but it does kinda explain why it happened.

It hasn't always been dreary and hopeless. At the start of last summer, my feet actually appeared to be in a decent condition. I'm not talking perfect – I had the occasional pain still, but they seemed to have recovered to what I felt was a pretty comfortable level. I'm talking the walking of many a mile without a penny of pain. But then came Glastonbury. Well, actually, before that came the disintegrating sole of my shoe. Over the course of about a week, I had knowingly watched different sections of the sole fall away without any thought as to how this might affect my feet. I'm not the best at buying new things; I like to leave stuff until it's a millimetre away from collapsing before acquiring a new version. This partly stems from a general dislike of buying and wasting fucktons of new stuff, but also because I'm fairly stingy with my money. I write that knowing that my mate Jack will latch onto it like a leech and search for his latest insult. This time though, my desire to save myself from further expenditure would have damaging results. Oblivious, I left uni in the land of Yorkshire puddings and returned home to the gentrified land of champagne socialists with the disintegrating soles upon my feet. The fact that I still hadn't realised that one of my shoes had effectively become lopsided might tell you that I'm not entirely fault-less in the demise of my feet. Oh well, they hadn't begun to hurt after a weekend of walking around Scarborough, so what more could Glastonbury do? I'd always have the essential spare pair of wellies to change into; great for your feet, if you hadn't guessed.

Glastonbury was more like the perfect storm for their collapse: day upon day of walking, night upon night of dancing, hour upon hour of standing bobbing along to the gentle sounds of Lekiddo Lord of the Lobsters. What a struggle, I know. It does become a bit of a struggle with lopsided shoes and fucked-up feet. I feel like these combinations are getting better and better. Considering my feet usually finish the festival in a dull aching state, doing it with sole-less shoes and actually injured feet was likely to create a bit more than a dull ache. According to their iPhone pedometers, the height of accuracy, many of my friends had walked and danced the equivalent of twenty-something miles per day. A couple of years ago *The Tab* brilliantly reported some fascinating news, as they always do – two guys had looked at their iPhones and realised they had walked four marathons in the five-day festival. I mean… what a story. So heavily researched, so intensely studied. Enough of the wondrous journalistic practices of today – I think you've got the point that there was to be a lot of walking in a short period of time.

I'm not sure if it was the dancing or the many miles of trudging about, but I woke up on the Saturday morning barely able to walk. Searing pain left me hobbling to the toilets whilst Mikey watched on from his camping chair, paralysed in permanent awe of Liam Gallagher. Wellies, strangely, appeared to be the less painful option of my shoe assortment. The huge clunkiness of their nature was not exactly approved of by the medic that I trekked halfway across the festival to see. If she'd seen my now decrepit alternative I think her opinion might have changed… Sympathetically, she revealed there was little that could be done at a festival like Glastonbury, camping down and sticking it out at a single stage for the day was probably my best option to not cause a further downfall. So, looking like a full-level twat with two pairs of socks and a pair of wellies, I marched out of the medic tent ready for the impending pain of the next two days.

Surprisingly, they never really got any worse over those two days. If I stood in certain ways the pain would temporarily subside, or just be overshadowed by the genius of Nile Rodgers and Chic. After many an hour aimlessly walking and singing, I ended the festival perched upon the top of Stone Circle Hill (a circle of stones on a hill, pretty self-explanatory). The old boys didn't feel dreadful, possibly because the pain was being disguised by the level of my intoxication. As I contemplated the past five days and the damage I had possibly done, huge cheers erupted across the hill – the sun had finally revealed itself from behind the opposite hill. Bright beams spread across our faces to the calming sounds of nitrous oxide being released into the air as fellow revellers delved into their last supplies of laughing gas. 'Chai tea! Chai tea! Chai tea!' bellowed a bearded man with a bucket full of the stuff. 'A pound for a cup,' he carried on, pushing the bucket on a makeshift pair of wheels from group to group, the sun shining down upon his back. It was a sight that only the hippy wonderland of Glastonbury could provide. A wonderland that had kind of fucked my feet over. At the time, I wasn't sure what the damage would be. I'd felt similarly in pain at the previous Glastonbury (I go every year because, despite the ever-rising price, it's my favourite place on earth) when the injury was fresher. Yet, that pain soon disappeared when I departed from the colossal level of mud that year. I pondered whether this year would be the same...

It wouldn't. The pain stuck around. Weirdly, it did disappear for a bit when I was walking a fuckton of miles around Europe (I wasn't hiking; I was just on holiday). But that was an anomaly. They've since set into their current slightly painful and what feels like permanent state. I have these occasional moments when I become inspired to put in some real effort in order to change that fact by returning to the stretches I thought I'd left behind. This inspired effort usually returns to the half-arsed acceptance of the current state of affairs rather quickly. It's not that I don't want to fix my feet; it's just that any effort that I seem to put in appears to have little impact. So, as you can guess, I get a bit demoralised. None of this really gets me down. I mean, I'd love to be jumping about, playing football, hiking across hills, running through wheat fields, but I'm OK with the fact that I can't. I hope that at some point over the next few years my feet will have recovered to the point where they can do such things with relative ease. For now though, I'm fairly comfortable in the knowledge that they can't and probably won't be able to for a while. At least I can dance the night away to occasionally half-decent music in my newly adopted home of York. If that was taken from me, I don't know what I'd do...

Probably lie aimlessly in bed, not too different from normal. My life at uni largely consists of either being surprisingly busy or just lying in my bed. This sounds lazy. It partly is. However, a lot of this lying occurs because I work best in that habitat. It's odd; sitting at a desk or on the sofa appears to limit my ability to work. I have to lie on my front, ever so attractively hunched up, or sit upright with my back against the wall to get anything done. Maybe it's because I'm some pretentious knob who can only write when they're in a specific place or position. I need to feel those springs jabbing against my bones to understand the deeper workings of my imagination. Nah. I just like it. It also makes it easy to collapse into a quick nap. Replenish that mind, you know.

All this lying about largely occurs because I now want to be a writer, not an actor. Definitely not an actor. Every time I read over this book, the weirdest part is reading my passionate embrace of acting, something that feels so distant now. The stage is no longer somewhere I feel comfortable – it's become a place infested with fear. My confidence, bit by bit, has drained away. I even get nervous performing in class. I'm not talking little nerves. I mean serious, anxiety-inducing nerves. The feeling that everyone's going to judge me because I'll stutter or perform a line like a wooden post. I don't know where it came from but, at some point in the last year, my belief in my acting ability disappeared. I become lost in my own mind, overthinking everything. An unconfident actor will never be a good actor. I have the utmost belief in that statement. Confidence changes a performance, and the loss of it has changed what I want to do with my life. I've come to the acceptance that I'm all right at acting. Not the worst in the world, but nothing special either. Put simply, you need to be better than all right to succeed. That, coupled with my lack of confidence, has led me to largely give up on my teenage dream and pursue a different path.

Writing. Play-writing to be specific. I haven't completely deserted theatre. I still want to exist within that world but as the person who creates it, not the one who brings it to life. I desperately needed some sort of purpose after coming to terms with reality, but that wasn't the only reason I turned to writing. I fell in love with it. I've always enjoyed creating these worlds, acting out every line I write whilst pacing around my room as if I embodied each character. It had helped sort out my acting withdrawals. But now, it's different. I love writing for the joy of what it is, not as some measly replacement for performing. Spending evenings, penned up in my room, thinking about the depth of relationship between Person A and Person B. The love, anger or hatred that may lie within it. Imagining this and putting it onto a piece of paper as fact. That's what I love. Even if a lot of the time it might be shit, the process, and the fact that I have created a whole world from nothing, provides me with pleasure. It still allows me to self-soothe; transferring my own emotions into the script is as therapeutic as pouring them into a character when acting. Arguably even more: I can now propel my emotions onto a wide variety of characters while having complete control over what emotions these are and to what level they are released. 'Complete control' makes me sound a bit like a control freak. Hiding away at the back to let someone else dictate what to do is a more fitting description. I've brushed over the fact that writing gives me purpose, but it is an essential benefit. It means that when I have days with nothing on or evenings which could easily be spent in front of the TV, I can fill them by writing. This helps when you're the kind of person who cannot lie about doing nothing all day because it makes you feel unproductive and pathetic. Basically, writing is what I want to do with my life and I love it.

I guess that's the one thing that my university course has definitely given me: the desire to be a playwright. I never saw myself as a writer for the big boy stage until I came to uni. Being here changed that. The course didn't directly do it, but it did bring my strongest focus to theatre and forced me to read more plays. So I gradually became acquainted with the idea of writing in a similar fashion. Aside from that, I'm not sure how much impact my course has had on me. I mean it's all right. That kind of summarises my life right now. All right. Uni's all right. Life's all right. Football's not all right but we won't speak about that. More importantly, I'm all right (well importantly to me, not sure you give much of a shit about it). I have my struggles. Everyone does. I've had bad moments since my year off, moments where I've felt a long way from happiness. But those were only moments, albeit sometimes quite prolonged moments, and for the large part I've enjoyed being at uni. Living independently in a completely different city far away from home: it's fun. I feel very settled in York now, it's that kind of place. I love it more than I ever thought I would. The city, not the uni, just to be clear. Like I said before, the uni's all right. But the city, that's a different story. I'm gonna let it have a whole paragraph because it is a beautiful and wondrous place.

I don't think anyone could hate York, to be honest. If you did, you'd have to be a right grumpy twat. It's heartwarming; it's charming; it's enchanting. On a regular basis I walk through the city and realise how much I adore it. Many sweet and charming things make me feel this way. The tiny winding cobbled streets that lie, almost secretly, within the city centre, losing you in a wonderland of confusion ('snickelways'). The fact that the River Ouse bursts its banks almost every two weeks, making leaving bars on the river ever more entertaining. The endearing nature of how tragic many of the clubs and bars within the city are; Popworld with its revolving dance floor may have to win it. The endless numbers of pubs (one for every day of the year, apparently) that mean a regular terraced street like the one next to mine has a sweet little drinking hole squished into its centre. Beautiful buildings on every street corner; I could go on. Give me an hour, and I'll bore your eyes out with a million more reasons for my love of this majestic city. I've lived here for over a year and still can't get over it. I'm happy here, living by the river, discovering new things. It's my home and I love it.

Just a quick clarification so that my friends and family don't get too offended: London is also my home and in a way it always will be, but a different kind of home. My childhood home. Where I grew up. It'll always be with me even if I won't always be with it.

Now, with that wishy-washy statement out the way, I feel it is a good time to depart from being with you. For real this time. I've enjoyed your imagined company as I've delved halfway into my mind (obviously I'm not gonna give you the whole thing – come on). But, yeah, thanks for delving into that half with me. This time I definitely won't be back.

Patrons

Sophia Akhtar
Babatunde Alabi
Paul Allcorn
Becca Armstrong
Max Ashby Holme
Will Ashcroft
Clem Ashton
Debbie Ashton
Isaac Atkin
James Austwick
Ken and Gill Austwick
Katherine Avery
Emily Bamford
Stephanie Barker
Renee Baure
Shabna Begum
Melissa Benn
Rachel Binnie
Ruby Bircher
Gizella Blackshaw
Kate Blackshaw
Ali Bomaye
Charles Boot
Lucy Booth
Simon Bradley
Alice Broadribb
Matthew Butler
Bethany Carricker
Kayleigh Chambers
Sean Clare
Rivka Cocker
Libbi Coldicott

Laura Corlett
Stuart Crainer
Paul Craven and Susan Cohen
Flo Davies
Sam Davies
Alison Deane
Suzanne Dekker
Gabriel Dentoni
Calum Dick-Oakley
Caroline Diehl
Les Dodd
Katy Driver
Maeve Dwyer
Henrik Edström
Rob Edwards
Jennifer Fleming
Jessica Forbes
Ed Foster
Su Fox
Iona Frith-Fletcher
James Galster
Ella Garrard
Tolga Goff
Skye and Bonnie Griffin
Ernie Griffith
Andrew Hall
Bunny Hankers
Alison Hardy
Isaac Hargreaves
Joseph Harvey
Ross Hayward
Elle Hibbert
Rebecca Hindle
Emma Holtom
Tamara Hopewell
Kim Hosking

Philip Hunt
Femi Hwesuhunu
Sam Jacobs
Iona Jacobson
Marion Janner
Matthew Jennings
Katie Jones
Mischa Jones
Samuel Joseph
Paul Kelland
Nathan Kohn
Carina Kvikstadhagen
Moonseok Kwak
Ed L
Tung Le
Maisie Leddy
Mollie Lisle
Benjamin Lowe
Karen Macleod
Henry Manthorpe
Nora Martin
Henry Mathias
Michael Maynard
Carole McIntosh
Luke McMahon
Ute Methner
Renae Miller
Ashley Milne
Philippa Milnes-Smith
Janis Mines
James Moir
Chris Morgan
Laura Moseley
Carlo Navato
Leanne Nguyen
Duncan Nottage

Abby O'Reilly
Nigel Paine
Jamie Paradise
Gareth Pedrick
Claire Perry
Christopher Phillips
David Porter
Nicola Powell
Louise Reeson
Mirain Rhisiart
Jamie Richards
Beatrice Rix
Alice Robb
Jessy Roberts
Chany Robinson
Eva Ruijgrok-Lupton
Angelo Russell
Meg Ryder
Matthew Searle
Helen Sharples
Clare Simmons
Alice Simpson
Beth Sitek
Tessalie Skoczylas
Alexi Smith
Ellis Southgate-Wilkinson
Helen Stanes
Henry Stewart
John Stewart
Lindsey Stewart
Theresa Stewart
Chris Stoddart
Nina Stutler
Carrie Supple
Stanley Swift
Mabel Taylor

Michael Taylor
Denon Thoresby
Lena Tondello
Juan Toro
Jamie Treanor
Lukas Truman
Diane Tuckey
Mia Tuckey
Sophie Tutaev
Sean Wallace
Diye Wariebi
Owen Watts Moore
Karlo Welch
Rosa Wells
Miranda Whiting
Francesca Wigley
Connor Wilkinson
Ben Wilson
Jo Winstanley
Sir Alan Wood